READI

FASTER!

---Making Molehills Out of Paper Mountains---

The

Intensive Reading Program

by

Richard K. Goetzman, Ph.D.

10 Easy Lessons for Mastering Reading Speed and Effectiveness

Revised Edition

Professional Resource Center

2028 17th Avenue NW

Rochester, MN 55901-1514

507/282-0941

This book is available at special discount rates when ordered in large quantities. For ordering information and pricing, contact the Professional Resource Center, 2028 17th Avenue NW, Rochester, MN 55901-1514, 507/282-0941.

Reading Better, Faster!
is an updated, revised edition of the previously
printed and copyrighted book
The Rapid Reader's Survival Manual.

Professional Resource Center

2028 17th Avenue NW

Rochester, MN 55901-1514

507/282-0941

ISBN 0-9633993-0-6

TABLE OF CONTENTS

(cont'd on next page)

Table of Contents—cont'd

"What we are is God's gift to us;
what we become is our gift to God!"

AUTHOR'S NOTE

---Welcome to Intensive Reading---

Summary:

1. Most people read at only 30-40% of their potential. The simple techniques needed to realize their full potential are not part of the traditional educational process.
2. As a solution to the problem, *Intensive Reading* was introduced in 1978. Since then, thousands of people have participated in *Intensive Reading* workshops with an average speed gain of over 150% and an ending speed average of over 600 wpm (words per minute).
3. *Intensive Reading* works for all types of reading—easy or difficult, entertainment or study.
4. This book will take you through the same effective steps presented at the workshop so that anyone who wants to become a faster, more effective reader can do so.
5. Once it is learned and reinforced through habitual use, *Intensive Reading* will stay with you for life.

Getting Acquainted:

In the 1960s, when I was teaching high school, I realized there must be some techniques that made one reader "better" than another. Having always been a "good" reader myself, I started analyzing my own reading skills and comparing them with others. I read book after book about reading techniques; and I took reading courses whenever I could find them. I also interviewed elementary school teachers and researched many of the common teaching methods in reading. The result was a firm conviction that most people utilize only 30-40% of their potential in both speed and efficiency. I also discovered that the techniques needed to realize this untapped literacy potential were extremely simple and quite easy to learn. They were not included, however, in the traditional school curriculum.

Over the years, a rash of educational-effectiveness studies reaffirmed my findings by listing the need for upgraded reading skills as the number one priority in education reform. The Information Age, in which we were so suddenly immersed, was giving us an explosion of raw data and knowledge that was absolutely phenomenal. An unbelievable proliferation of printed material threatened to bury us all unless we learned to process it through finely-tuned, advanced literacy skills. Since the schools did not deal with the problem effectively, I decided it was time to find a solution. I put all of my research information together with my experiences in education and came up with a simple format of several basic techniques that soon proved to be extremely effective in teaching advanced literacy to just about anyone. The methodology I developed was called *Intensive Reading*, and I began teaching it at various corporate training seminars. The results were immediate and dramatic.

In the first half of the *Intensive Reading* workshop, students were taught new reading concepts and simple speed-enhancement techniques (the primary tool being an effective pacing method). In the second half of the program, students learned techniques for using this speed most effectively in various types of material, from fiction to technical, from entertainment to study. These techniques included organizing reading material for fast, effective processing via the *Organized Reading System*, learning to be selective in the reading process by spending time only on material that satisfied needs, and using an effective "Read first—Learn second" technique, the *Margin Code System*.

The program worked well from the very start and thousands of students have, over the years, averaged reading speed gains of over 150%. With a mean incoming speed of 267 words per minute and a mean ending rate of 660 wpm, they were reading over two and a half times faster in just a few hours.

Over the intervening years, there have been hundreds of classes and thousands of successful readers. The most common question I heard from these thousands of successful "Intensive" readers was, "This is so easy to learn! Why don't they teach it in the schools?" I had no good answer for them. I had made repeated offers to schools, both private and public, to do an *Intensive Reading* program for them (even offering it as a no-charge, pilot study) and had been rejected every time. The routine response was, "We already teach reading." The accuracy (or inaccuracy) of that reply remains at the very heart of the illiteracy issue.

A glimmer of hope did appear in the summer of 1991, when Linda L., a third grade teacher from St. Felix Grade School (Wabasha, MN), asked me if there might be some way we could incorporate my techniques in her classroom. After talking with her and a wonderfully enthusiastic principal, we set up a pilot program. Once a week, for eight weeks, I met for an hour and a half with 27 eager third graders. During the course of the school days between my visits, Linda reinforced the learning with drills and exercises as well as regular use of the techniques in all their reading across the curriculum. The results were outstanding—the speeds attained by these youngsters were phenomenal and, at the same time, comprehension improved significantly. Using the National Achievement Test just before we started the eight-week study and then using it again after the eight weeks, we saw the average percentile ranking rise from 51 to 84. That's a gain of more than 60%. The program was an unqualified success in the minds of the teacher, the students, the parents, and the school. I am hoping that this pilot class will lead the way to many more similar school programs. The walls have been breached!

The second most common question I have been asked is, "How can I get this program for my husband/wife/child/etc.?" This book is the answer to that question. With this ten-lesson, self-study manual, you do not have to be an employee of a corporation that is providing the workshop as part of its continuing education program; nor do you have to be a member of an association or organization that is providing a workshop for its members; nor do you have to attend a public seminar. All you have to do is follow the directions carefully. This revised and improved edition of the manual makes it even easier for you to learn the *Intensive Reading Program.* The lessons and exercises will lead you very quickly and very effectively to a greatly-enhanced reading skill of high speed and efficiency.

There are no short cuts to *Intensive Reading.* Your first step is to read the Introduction with care since it will tell you just how to use this book most effectively. If you do a good job of reading the Introduction, and, if you follow all of the directions, you will soon find yourself reading at speeds that will truly amaze you. Your confidence will grow enormously and your enjoyment of reading will be enhanced significantly. You will see your self-esteem grow, too, as you affirm your own individuality and find great success in this very rewarding area of self-improvement.

So, on to the Introduction! You are already started on the path to high-speed, efficient reading—a skill that will serve you in good stead for the rest of your life. Thousands of people—of all ages, at all educational levels, from all walks of life—have done it before you; you can do it, too!

Richard K. Goetzman, Ph.D.

---"The Reading Doctor"---

"We cannot direct the wind,
but we can adjust the sails!"

INTRODUCTION

---How To Use This Book---

Summary:

1. To get the full benefit of the *Intensive Reading Program*, you must follow the directions very closely.
   - Do not skip ahead and do not shortcut.
   - Set aside a specific time to study.
   - Do one lesson a day or one lesson every other day.
2. You will need to prepare ahead of time to see that you have the necessary books and materials for each lesson.
3. These lessons are short and the drills are easy if you take them step by step.
4. In just a short time you will see your confidence grow as your speed rises dramatically.

Getting Maximum Benefits:

You will find that the maximum benefits from *Intensive Reading* will occur only if you follow the directions closely and carefully. There are no shortcuts. If you try to work out of sequence and do only selected parts of the program, you will be selling yourself and *Intensive Reading* short. Each step of each lesson has been designed with the ultimate goal of rapid, effective reading in mind. Considering that most people read somewhere between 150 and 350 wpm (which is only 30-40% of their potential), you can look forward to a dramatic increase in your reading speed. A realistic objective is to at least double your speed or end up at over 500 wpm. Many people far exceed this expectation.

Years of research, planning, adapting and editing went into this book to make it as easy as possible for you to attain high reading speeds. It is entirely up to you to put these simple techniques to work. You will have to set aside time each day to read the lessons and do the drills. In a very short time, the results will exhilarate you and you will come to realize that the effort is well worth it. A few hours of dedication to this simple program of self-improvement will make you a rapid reader for the rest of your life. You will come to expect speed as a natural and necessary part of your reading process.

Setting a Schedule:

The first thing you must decide is just how quickly you want to complete the program and how much time you are willing to schedule regularly for this purpose.

- **One Lesson Per Day**—The lessons are set up so that you can easily do one lesson per day and complete the entire program in just ten days. If you set aside just one hour each day for the next ten days, you will find a lifetime of reading enjoyment waiting at the end of those ten hours.
- **One Lesson Every Other Day**—If time is *truly* a problem, you may do one lesson every other day. This will still get you through the program in less than three weeks.
- **Splitting Lessons**—Lessons 2, 3, 5, 7, 9 and 10 are primarily drilling; and each should definitely be done in a single session. Lessons 1, 4, 6, and 8, however, are "content" or "learning" lessons and may be split in half if you desire. What this means is that each of these content lessons introduces you to a new *Intensive Reading* concept or technique with a complete discussion and explanation so you can understand it thoroughly. The lesson then goes on to introduce you to some drills that will make use of the information you have just learned. If you wish, you may split each of these four learning lessons into two parts—first, the explanation; second, the drilling. This approach will add only four days to your overall schedule.
- **Overdoing It**—Do not try to complete two lessons a day in order to speed up the process. The program is specifically designed for no more than one lesson per study session. If you try to do more, you will not allow your brain to assimilate the information and techniques you have just learned. You will experience information overload which results in too much confusion and frustration. Your extra

effort will actually become counterproductive. Be patient. In just a short time, your perseverance will be amply rewarded.

- **Goal Setting**—It is of primary importance that you establish an absolute goal for yourself, setting aside the time to do the lessons on a regular basis (daily or every other day); and, then, sticking to your schedule with no exceptions. An hour a day (or every other day) may seem like an enormous commitment at first, but it pales as an investment measured against the time you will save over an entire lifetime of efficient reading. Resolve right now to become an *Intensive Reader.*

Environment:

The environment in which you do your lessons is extremely important. It can hinder or help the process. Here are some guidelines to a good study environment.

- **Place**—The best place to do your *Intensive Reading* is in a quiet room away from all distractions. Use a desk or table with a large enough area for your books, timer, paper, etc. Use a comfortable, straight-backed chair with good lower-back support. Bright, indirect lighting is the best—something that will neither glare nor cast shadows on the books.
- **Music**—People have often asked me, "What about music? I study better with my music playing in the background." To a degree, research bears out the theory that music helps one study. While generally valid, the theory has a few caveats. What many of the studies have concluded is that listening to your favorite music will help you relax and you will *seem* to be more attentive to what you are doing. However, retention of information learned with music is directly related to the type of music being played. If you use the wrong kind of music, you will have a very short retention of new information (in many cases as short as one day). Conversely, if you use the right kind of music, retention time can be significantly extended and learning actually enhanced. Basically, the music should be soft and sedate with no lyrics. Do not even use an instrumental version of a song that has lyrics because your brain will supply those lyrics as the music plays. This puts you into the predicament

of trying to do two things—read and "sing"—at one time. This means neither task will be done efficiently.

Some classical and some very new music is ideal. Here are some representative selections:

Pachalbel's "Canon"

Bach's "Brandenburg Concertos"

Handel's "Water Music"

Vivaldi's "Four Seasons"

Most any other Baroque music

+

Lynch's "Deep Breakfast"

Rowland's "The Fairy Ring"

Kitaro's "The Light of the Spirit"

Mannheim Steamroller's "Fresh Aire" series

Many "new age" or "Hearts of Space" compositions with harp, flute, guitar, etc.

(For a detailed study on the use of music in the learning process, see *Super Learning* by Ostrander & Schroeder.)

Lesson Procedures:

Here is an effective strategy that works best in doing each lesson/chapter. These steps to effective learning will be explained in detail when you get to Lesson 6.

- Overview—Start each lesson by paging through the chapter first to see how long it is and to note what sections it contains.
- Preview—Read the summary at the very beginning of the lesson to get a preview of the information being presented.
- Read—After prereading the lesson go on to actually reading the chapter and doing the recommended drills.
- Postview—Finally, quickly reread the summary to tie everything together and to reinforce what you have learned.

When you have been exposed to all the concepts of *Intensive Reading* you will understand exactly why this procedure is used. Remember that there are no shortcuts—follow all the steps of the lesson protocol just as prescribed above!

Preparation:

You will note that each lesson ends with a reminder of the books and materials you will need for the next lesson. Be sure to take careful note of this information so you have the needed items on hand before you begin the lesson. This means that you will finish each lesson by preparing for the following lesson. Don't wait until you start a lesson to see if you have what you need. If something is missing, you may be tempted to try the lesson without it, or you will have to stop what you are doing and get whatever is required. In either case you will disrupt the easy flow of the program and you will waste a lot of time. And, isn't effective use of your time one of the factors involved in your decision to learn to read faster?

Materials Needed:

There are a few items you will need throughout the *Intensive Reading Program* to help you do the drills and exercises. Prepare by having them all on hand before you even begin the first lesson.

- **Timer**—Throughout the ten lessons, you will be checking the timing of your drills or measuring your reading speed which will be recorded on your progress record (Appendix 3). The best device you can use for the timing is a digital, battery-operated kitchen timer. If you don't already own one, go out and invest a few dollars. You can use the timer for your *Intensive Reading* and get double duty with it in your kitchen. Wind-up timers are not suitable because they are not accurate enough for the shorter timings used in the drills and exercise. A watch or clock won't work because they require your constantly looking at them to check the time. This interrupts the designed flow of the drill procedures. You need a timer that will count down from a preset time and then beep when the time is up.

- **Stationery Supplies**—You might also want to have on hand a pencil, some scratch paper and a few paper clips. Small plastic clips seem to work the best because they don't have the tendency to snag the pages as the wire ones do when you use them to mark your place in the book.
- **Pace Card**—You will also need a pace card or two. A pace card is a blank card roughly the size of a business card. If you have old business cards, use them blank side up; if not, you can cut 3" x 5" cards in halves or thirds. If you are the kind of person who likes everything as precise as possible, the ideal size for general use is a 4" x 2" pace card. The exact size of the card, however, is not of critical importance. Just how you will use these cards will be explained shortly.
- **Calculator**—Since you will be making several calculations in order to compute your speed or wpp (words per page), you may want to use a small calculator if your multiplication or long division skills are a bit rusty.

Glossary:

In the back of this book is a glossary of some commonly used terms in *Intensive Reading.* Make good use of this section by taking a quick look at it before you begin the lessons and again when you need to remind yourself of some of the exact meanings of the specific terms.

Books You Will Need:

You will have to choose a few books for use in the drilling exercises and for computing your beginning and ending speeds. Initially, you will need only two books—one to be used for checking your reading speed on a regular basis in order to chart your progress, and one to use for the first few drills. You will need the first book (your "progress" book) immediately in order to calculate your Beginning Reading Rate. You will need the "drilling" book when you move on to Lesson 1. Refer to Appendices 1 and 2 right now for information on how to choose and use these books.

When you get to Lesson 8, you will need a couple of magazines of the type you normally read. *Reader's Digest* is an ideal selection.

Establishing Your Beginning Reading Rate:

In order to determine your Beginning Reading Rate, you will need to use the book you selected (per Appendix 1) as your "progress" book. This book should be used only in charting your progress and not for daily drilling. Then, using Appendix 2, you should have calculated the word counts for your book selections. You must also have on hand the digital timer mentioned earlier. When these three things (books, word count, and timer) are taken care of, you may proceed.

- **Step 1**—Before you do anything else, read all of the steps in this section. Only after reading the entire section should you proceed to actually doing Step 2, below.
- **Step 2**—Preread your book by looking at the jacket or cover information and by reading any introductory text that might lead you into the story.
- **Step 3**—Open the book to the first page of Chapter 1 and set your timer for three minutes.
- **Step 4**—Start the timer and immediately start reading. Read at a rate that gives you satisfactory comprehension, a rate that is "normal" for you in this kind of a book. Don't race, and don't drag your feet. Just relax and read as you normally would. When the timer signals the end of the three minutes, mark the last complete line you have read. Then proceed to the next step.
- **Step 5**—Get out a pencil and paper (and calculator, if you want) and do your arithmetic.

  ➡ Count the number of complete pages you have read and multiply by the average number of words per page as determined by the directions in Appendix 2.

  ➡ On the partial page(s) count the number of full lines you have read and multiply by the average number of words per line as determined by the directions in Appendix 2.

  ➡ Add these two figures together to get the total number of words read and then divide by three. The result will be your reading rate in wpm.

For example, after choosing your book (Appendix 1), you counted words (Appendix 2). You determined there was an average of 9 wpl (words per line) and an average of 300 wpp (words per page). In your three minute reading, you read the first page which was not a complete page because of the title, you read the second page which was complete, and you ended part way down the third page. Count full pages first: 1 x 300 = 300. Then count lines on the partial pages: if there were 25 lines on page one and you ended up on line 18 of page three, you'd have 25 + 18 = 43 lines total. 43 lines x 9 wpl = 387 words. Adding all the words together: 300 + 387 = 687. 687 divided by your total time of 3 minutes = 229 wpm.

Full pages x words per page = xxx words

Lines on partial pages x words per line = xxx words

total words

divide by 3

WPM

- **Step 6**—Record your speed in your "Personal Progress Record," Appendix 3, on the line "Beginning rate."
- **Step 7**—Mark your ending spot carefully with a paper clip or a bookmark and pencil check so that the next time you come back to this book for a progress reading you will be able to start at the exact spot where you left off. If, after you have computed your Beginning Reading Rate, you want to finish reading the paragraph or page just to make the placemarking easier, by all means do so.

Time-Out:

After assessing your beginning speed, you may want to stop and take a breather—you have done a lot so far just getting ready for the program. This set-up time will prove to be well worth the effort. It will make your lessons move so much more smoothly by having all the logistics taken care of in advance. If you have the time and the inclination, you may want to move right on to Lesson 1.

Preparing for Lesson 1:

To be fully prepared to do Lesson 1, you should have the following items on hand.

- Pace card(s)
- Progress book (just used above)
- Timer
- Drill book (light fiction per Appendix 1). Be sure to have the word counts done in advance (per Appendix 2).
- Paper clips
- Pencil and paper
- Calculator (optional)

"Why bother to carry a knife if it isn't sharp?"

"All things are possible
to those who believe!"

LESSON 1

---Learning to Pace---

Summary:

1. The reading process involves three distinct physical/mental factors.
   - **Fixations** are the stops your eyes make to take in a certain number of words which you say to yourself as you see them. This "self-talk" is called *subvocalization* or *auditory reassurance.*
   - **Duration** is the length of time your eyes dwell on those words.
   - **Regressions** are non-productive eye stops and diversions. They can be conscious as well as subconscious.
2. Each of these three factors is affected when you use an efficient pacing method such as card-pacing.
   - You take in more words per fixation.
   - The duration of those fixations is shortened.
   - Regressions are reduced to an insignificant frequency.
3. Drilling differs from reading in that drilling does not demand satisfactory comprehension.
4. Read through and then do Drill 1.
5. Measure and record your progress.

The Reading Process:

Before you can begin to tackle the job of improving your reading efficiency, you must understand the process of reading. This is not going to be a complicated laboratory analysis. We'll simply discuss it in a language that is very easy to understand. You'll be introduced to some new terms and definitions that will help you throughout the *Intensive Reading Program.* Remember the admonition that will be repeated many times, "Read first—Learn second," i.e., don't try to memorize as you read. Simply read this chapter and understand what you are reading *as* you read it without trying to "learn" it. The terms and definitions will be repeated often enough in future chapters that you will have an automatic reinforcement to your learning process. If you follow directions and do the drills properly, everything will fall into place just right. Don't try to *make* the system work, *let* it work!

Fixations:

When you read, it seems that your eyes move smoothly from left to right on each line and so on down the page line by line. But your eyes are not really moving that fluidly. They are stopping and starting constantly. They look at a small group of words then move on to the next group and the next group, etc. It is very similar to the movie process. When you are watching a movie, you do not see fluid movement. What you really see is a series of rapidly projected still pictures that give the impression of fluid movement. So it is with your eyes when you read. They stop, fixate on a group of words, and move on to the next group of words so rapidly that you get the feeling of fluid movement. Each one of these eye stops is called a "*fixation*." Normally, a fixation will take in from two to six words. A few readers may see only one word per fixation while others may see more than six. Most commonly, however, the average reader's eye span will take in three or four words per fixation.

Oral/Aural Reading:

As you stop and see the words at each fixation, you tend to say them silently to yourself. This saying the words to yourself is called "*subvocalization*." You also "hear" them which is called "*auditory reassurance*." Subvocalization is not an imperative part of the reading process; but, since English is a phonological language, i.e., it has specific sounds for its alphabet characters, we generally depend on those sounded-out words for our reading (even though we do it silently). This self-talk process is called "*oral/aural*" reading because, in our minds, we say *(oral)* and hear *(aural)* the words as we read them. The fastest we can subvocalize is between 600 and 800 wpm. A few people will get a little higher with practice, but 800 wpm is generally considered the top speed for most oral/aural reading.

Visual Reading:

Reading, however, can be done without subvocalization. This type of reading is called "*visual reading*," wherein the reader sees the words and they are automatically converted to ideas and concepts without going through the subvocalization stage. A musician does much the same thing when reading music. The musician sees the notes which are automatically transferred by the brain into motor signals which, in turn, cause the musician to produce that particular set of notes on the instrument. Musicians do not consciously say each note to themselves as they play. Can you imagine what a symphony orchestra would sound like if each musician took the time to say each note silently before playing it? There would be an unbelievable cacophony!

The same general process occurs when a secretary, who has just typed a letter flawlessly, is asked about the letter's content and she replies, "I don't know. I didn't read it." What she doesn't realize is that she did in fact read it—*visually*! What she really meant to say was that she couldn't recall what she'd read because she hadn't subvocalized each word and she hadn't trained herself to recall visually-read material. Visual reading demands speeds over 1200 wpm (too fast to even try to subvocalize). Getting rid of the subvocalization habit to become a visual reader is an extremely lengthy, difficult, regimented process. Those who read visually tend to level off around 1600 wpm, although there is a wide range of readers who go much faster—upwards of 8,000 wpm. Once achieved, visual reading speeds are quickly lost if not used continually. We are not going to worry about visual reading in these *Intensive Reading* lessons except to recognize its existence and understand its meaning when we mention it later on.

Duration:

The next factor we must understand is "duration." Duration is the length of each fixation. It is the time we take to look at three or four words, subvocalize them, think about them, and move on to the next fixation. The duration of most readers' fixations will vary roughly from 20/100 of a second to 60/100 of a second. As far as the brain is concerned, this is a lot of time.

Over thirty years ago, subliminal researchers found out that a pictorial or verbal message could be flashed on a screen slow enough for the *subconscious* mind to see and react to but too fast for the *conscious* mind to even realize it was there. It was, in turn, discovered that the average person could see and react to a four or five word phrase in 1/100 of a second. If you do a little careful calculating you will see that this means that the brain has the potential to read *visually* between 24,000 and 30,000 wpm. This is mentioned only to give you an idea of the possibilities that exist and to show you that you can move down the page much faster than you are accustomed to going. Simply keep this information in mind until we tie it all together shortly.

Regressions:

The third factor we must recognize is *regression*. In *Intensive Reading* terminology, a regression is any eye movement that does not progress to the next sequential group of words. While this regression is sometimes conscious, it is more often subconscious wherein we are not even aware we are doing it. After fixing on a group of three or four words and before moving on to the next group of words in sequence, our eyes may stray unconsciously to look back at something in the previous paragraph or sentence, glance out the window, check the water in the glass to see how much is left, flit to the top of the page to look at the page number, check the time on the clock, look down the page to see what's coming up, etc. The problem with these regressions is that they happen while our minds are concentrating on what we are reading and, very often, we are totally unaware they are happening.

Let's illustrate with a similar phenomenon. You finish lunch and go back to work. You have a meeting in two hours so you decide to get some paperwork done in the meantime. You are working on the papers, take a quick look at your watch to check the time, and go back to the paperwork. A co-worker interrupts with, "Hey, what time was that?" And what do you do? That's right! You look at your watch again to get the time. You know you had just looked at your watch but you can't recall what you saw; so, you have to look again. What happened was that you "read" your watch visually—you didn't subvocalize. Your *subconscious* brain knew the time, but your *conscious* mind didn't.

This is exactly how regressions work. Your eyes flit around subconsciously looking at different things while your conscious brain is involved with thinking about the material you are reading. You don't even realize the regressions are happening. These regressions occur very erratically, but, over a period of time, average out to one regression for every three or four fixations. The duration of a regression is about the same as of a fixation. Thus, you can see that 1/4 or 1/5 of your time is wasted on unneeded regressions. Hold this information in abeyance while we learn about our first reading technique, pacing.

Pacing's Undeserved Bad Image:

Throughout our reading lives, we have learned and been reminded many times (either explicitly or implicitly), "Don't point to the words with your finger while you read." Traditional reading methodologies decry the use of "finger pointing" for "normal" readers; yet, they turn around and use finger pointing as a primary tool for teaching reading to dyslexics and learning-disabled children. If it works for these youngsters, why not for everyone else?

Think about it for a moment. If I give you a dictionary and ask you to look up a word, what are you most likely to do to make it easier to find the definition? Of course! You'll run your finger down the page to help isolate the word you are looking for. And, if I ask you to look up a phone number, how do you do that? More than likely you will run your finger down the page as an aid to finding the name and number. Sometimes you may use a pencil or a ruler or whatever else is handy to guide your eyes down the page, but the point is that *you use some kind of pacing device to keep your eyes on the task at hand.* By pacing in some way—finger, pencil, etc.—you find you are much more efficient in the search process. Why? Here's what's happening.

Pacing's True Image—An Efficient Reading Tool:

When you use an efficient pacing method (which we'll introduce in just a minute) you affect each of the three reading factors.

- **Regressions**—The first and most significant effect of efficient pacing is the reduction of regressions to near zero. You will never do away with regressions completely, but you will reduce them to an insignificant number. For all practical purposes, they will be eliminated.

- **Fixations**—The next gain from proper pacing is a reduction in the number of fixations needed. As you pace, you force your eyes to move in a more determined pattern and you can move much more rapidly than you did without pacing. What happens is that your eyes do not just move faster, they move smarter by taking in more words every time they stop. This is a totally subconscious process—don't try to *make* it happen, just *let* it happen. When you pace correctly, your eyes tend to widen their span and take in more words every time they stop. An average reader might well take in four words per fixation with good pacing instead of three with no pacing technique. That would mean fewer stops for any given amount of material. And fewer stops means faster overall speed.
- **Duration**—Through a proper pacing technique, our eyes are encouraged to reduce the amount of time they dwell on any one fixation. After all, if, as we learned earlier, the eyes and brain really need only 1/100 of a second for a four or five word phrase, surely the average reader's 50/100 of a second is an unnecessarily long time for looking at just a few words. In the pacing process, the eyes seem to work on their own and act with *subconscious* efficiency by reducing the time they dwell on each fixation. The average reader can expect to see at least a 20% reduction in duration time. Remember the earlier admonition, "Don't try to make it happen; let it happen!"

What an Average Reader Gains:

To see how all these factors work together to give enormous speed gains, let's take a look at an average reader before and after pacing. Before pacing, an average reader with a speed of 270 wpm would have a profile something like this:

90 fixations + 30 regressions = 120 eye stops

120 stops at .50 seconds each = 60 seconds

(90 + 30) x .50 = 60

After learning proper pacing methods, however, the profile would be:

68 fixations + 00 regressions = 68 eye stops

68 stops at .40 seconds each = 27 seconds

68 x .40 = 27

By using proper pacing techniques, the reader finished in just 27 seconds what had previously taken 60 seconds. Speed has increased from 270 wpm to 600 wpm, a noteworthy 122% gain. In other words, the reader is now reading more than twice as fast simply by learning to pace properly. It is a tremendous gain for such a simple technique.

The key to effective pacing is doing it correctly and doing it ***ALWAYS!***

How to Pace Properly:

If you were a beginning reader, the first step to good reading habits would be to use your finger to point to each word as you struggled to pronounce and read it. But, because you already read at a functional level, we will skip the beginning and intermediary steps that lead to the method we will use from now on—*card pacing.*

Remember, in the introduction, you were asked to have some blank cards on hand? Well, we'll use them now! It makes no difference if you are using the suggested 4" x 2" card, a business card, a cut down 3" x 5" card, or even a full 3" x 5" card. Take a card in one hand (whichever hand you feel most comfortable using), hold the card in a horizontal position between thumb and fingers (yes, actually do it now) and pace down the page of this book as you are reading these words. Imagine you are very lightly scraping off the words you have just read. *The card must come down the page from above the lines you are reading.*

From now on, every time you read, no matter when or what you are reading, you must use the card as a pacer. You must make pacing a habit; and that can be done only through constant, repeated practice. Please don't make the mistake of thinking it is something you can just turn on and turn off simply because you know about it. *It must be made a habit!*

The key to making this pace card technique work effectively is to make sure you are coming down from above the lines you are reading. There are two distinct advantages to using the pace card this way.

With the card above the line you are reading, you eliminate the possibility of your eyes flitting back to reread something. This type of regression is sometimes conscious and sometimes unconscious; but, in either case, it is usually caused by an unwarranted lack of confidence in your ability to "comprehend" or an attempt on your part to "learn" (memorize) as you read. When we discuss comprehension, later, in Lesson 4, you will see how all these factors tie into effective reading techniques and what is meant by the admonition to "Read first—Learn second." For now, just accept the premise that the card from above will help you, and checking back on just-read material is really not necessary.

The second, and perhaps more important, value of using the pace card from above is that it allows you to take advantage of your peripheral vision. Let's use an analogy. When you drive, you have a "hard" focus a certain distance in front of your car. Yet, your brain takes in all kinds of peripheral information that you really don't pay much attention to until action is needed. You speed up, slow down, move left or right according to this peripheral information that your brain takes in subconsciously. A great share of the time, you don't even think about it; you just do it.

When you read with a pace card, allowing your eyes to see ahead, you get the same subconscious peripheral advantage, i.e., you speed up, slow down, etc. according to the "traffic" up ahead. You do not have to be consciously aware that you are doing it; it just happens.

Final Note:

The *Intensive Reading Program* is designed with a very purposeful sequence in mind. The techniques you are learning will fall into place as you progress through the lessons. Thousands of people have done it before you, so be confident in your ability do it, too. If you approach the ensuing drills and lessons with a positive, confident attitude, you will be very pleasantly surprised at how easy it is to improve your speed dramatically.

Drilling:

Before we actually move on to the first drill, let's take just a few moments to discuss some general concerns about drilling. An absolute requirement is that you separate *drilling* from *reading.*

- **Reading** is pacing through material at the fastest possible rate that will still allow for adequate comprehension. (You get what you need to get from the material.)
- **Drilling** is pacing through material at a speed faster than will allow for adequate comprehension. When you drill, you you do not need nor do you even want adequate comprehension. *If you are getting satisfactory comprehension, you are going too slow.*

The purpose of the first few drills is to get you acclimated to the pacing technique and to get your raw speed moving upwardly very quickly. You must always drill at a speed faster than you would normally read. If you were to drill at your normal reading speed, you would only reinforce what you are already doing and no progress would result. Push for speed right from the beginning.

Set your mind at ease by recognizing that *speed comes first, then comprehension.* If you try to make comprehension a part of the speed drills you will only frustrate yourself and waste a lot of time. By learning to do these early drills properly, comprehension *will* follow. You cannot force it. (By the way, are you using your pace card right now? It's an absolute requirement, remember!)

Keep reminding yourself you are drilling to learn the pacing techniques—content is totally immaterial at this point. Don't be overanxious to make everything happen at once. After all, if you do one lesson a day as prescribed, you will finish in just ten days with a new reading efficiency that will make you very proud. Remember, we are talking about speeds at the top of the subvocalization range, 600—800 wpm. Less than 1/2 of 1 percent of the literate adults in the United States can read at those speeds; and you can be one of them in less than two weeks. It's up to you. You can do it!

Lesson 1 Drill:

- **Preparation**—Make sure you have made all the necessary preparations for the drill. Have at hand your timer, drill book, paper, pencil, clips, and the pace card as described in the Introduction.

- **Drilling**—Go, now, to the back of this book and read all of Drill 1. Reread if necessary to be sure you understand how to do it. Then, actually do Drill 1.
- **Progress Record**—One of the things you did as you followed directions in the Introduction, was to take a three minute reading in a work of light fiction we labeled "progress" book. After doing the above-prescribed drill, use that progress book starting wherever you left off at the end of that first timed reading ("Beginning Reading Rate"), set your timer, and read for three minutes using the pace card. Be sure you are using your pace card! Push yourself at *your best rate*—your fastest speed that still allows for *adequate comprehension*. You are to be *reading* not *drilling*.

➡ At the end of the three minutes, mark your place and compute your speed just as you did earlier in the Introduction for the "Beginning Rate."

Full pages x words per page = xxx words

Lines on partial pages x words per line = xxx words

total words

divide by 3

WPM

➡ Mark your speed on the progress chart in Appendix 3, on the line, "Lesson 1." You should see a rise in speed after just one short lesson and drill. Remember, it is very early in the program—you have just barely started. Think of what you stand to gain after you've completed the full program! With this encouraging sign, resolve to put concerted effort into the remaining lessons.

Preparing for the Next Lesson:

When you have done Drill 1 and a progress check as directed, you are almost finished for the day. Very quickly, make sure you are ready for Lesson 2. If you prepare your next lesson now, you will find it much easier to proceed when the time comes to actually do it. Be ready by having the following items on hand.

- Pace card
- Timer
- Progress book
- Drill book (light non-fiction—word counts complete)
- Clips
- Scratch paper
- Pencil
- Calculator (optional)

"Beware of the person of one book!"

"Believe in failure and you will be right
for you will indeed fail.
Believe in success and again you will be right
for you will indeed succeed.
It is, therefore, to your distinct advantage
to believe in success!"

LESSON 2

---Pacing Drills and Reinforcement---

Summary:

1. The concepts you learned in Lesson 1 must be reviewed and then reinforced with more drilling.
2. Do the "Vertical Pacing Exercise" contained in Appendix 4.
3. Do Drill 1, as in Lesson 1.
4. Read, then do Drill 2.
5. Measure and record your progress.
6. Look at your gains *overall*, rather than comparing each individual day to the next.

Prereading:

Do everything exactly as directed. Be sure to read through the entire lesson, *then* come back and do the prescribed tasks. Make sure you have all needed items on hand before you begin the drill. Think of yourself as an accomplished reader who is getting better and better every day. This is exactly what is happening!

Review and Reinforcement:

1. In Lesson 1, you learned about the elements of fixations, duration, and regressions and how they are affected by proper pacing. Stop for just a minute to review what you remember about these factors. If you feel fairly certain that you understand them clearly, you are ready to proceed. If you are not quite sure, go back to Lesson 1 and do a quick sweep-through (pacing) of the chapter. Be sure to use your pace card, of course, just as you surely are doing right now! (Remember, *you must use the pace card every time you read!*)

2. Turn to Appendix 4 in the back of the book and follow the directions for doing the "Vertical Pacing Exercise."

3. Do Drill 1, following the directions just as you did in Lesson 1. Be sure to read through the drill procedures quickly before you actually do the drill.

4. Preread, then do, Drill 2. This is a new drill for you, so follow the directions carefully.

5. Make another progress check using your "progress" book. Starting wherever you left off at the end of your last timed reading, set your timer for three minutes, and read at your "best" rate using the pace card. ***Be sure you are using your pace card!*** Push yourself at whatever you feel is your fastest speed that will still allow adequate comprehension. You are *reading* not *drilling*.

   At the end of the three minutes, mark your place and compute your speed just as you did before.

Full pages x words per page = xxx words

Lines on partial pages x words per line = xxx words

total words

divide by 3

WPM

6. Mark this calculated speed on the progress chart in Appendix 3, on the line, "Lesson 2."

Analyzing Gains:

Don't try to analyze the value of each day's gain by comparing it to the day before. There are many factors that can influence your speed and give you an erratic growth pattern, i.e., up one day, down the next. If you have this erratic pattern, don't fret about it. It's the *overall change* that we are concerned with. You *will* see this growth over the long run.

Preparing for the Next Lesson:

When you have done the drills and a progress check as directed, you are almost finished for the day. Very quickly, make sure you are ready for Lesson 3. If you prepare your next lesson now, you will find it much easier to proceed when the time comes to actually do it. Be ready by having these items on hand:

- Pace card.
- Timer.
- "Progress" book.
- Drill book (light non-fiction with word counts complete).
- Clips.
- Scratch paper.
- Pencil.
- Calculator (optional).

"Every expert was once a beginner!"

"It's never too late to be
what you might have been!"

LESSON 3

---Speed Drills and Reinforcement---

Summary:

1. The concepts that you learned in Lesson 1 and practiced in Lesson 2 must be reviewed and then reinforced with more drilling.
2. Read through, then do Drill 3.
3. Do *either* Drill 1 or 2.
4. Measure and record your progress.

Prereading:

Do everything exactly as directed. Be sure to read through the entire lesson, *then* come back and do the prescribed tasks. Make sure you have all needed items on hand before you begin the drills. Keep reminding yourself that every expert was once a beginner and you are that beginner on the road to becoming an accomplished reader.

Review and Reinforcement:

1. In Lesson 1 you learned about pacing and its effect on your reading speed. Then you did a drill to help you learn how to pace. Lesson 2 required you to do two drills that continued this reinforcement of the pacing technique. If you need a review of the procedures presented in Lesson 1, go back and do a very rapid review of the chapter to make sure you have the concepts locked in solidly.
2. Carefully read through the directions for Drill 3. After you have read through the drill and understand the procedure, do the drill.
3. Choose either Drill 1 or 2, read through it quickly to refresh yourself on the procedure, then actually do the drill.
4. Make another progress check using your "progress" book. Starting wherever you left off at the end of your last timed reading, set your

timer for three minutes, and read at your "best" rate using the pace card. ***Be sure you are using your pace card!*** Push yourself at whatever you feel is your fastest speed that will still allow adequate comprehension. You are now *reading* not *drilling*.

At the end of the three minutes, mark your place and compute your speed just as you did before.

Full pages x words per page = xxx words

Lines on partial pages x words per line = xxx words

total words

divide by 3

WPM

5. Mark this calculated speed on the progress chart in Appendix 3, on the line, "Lesson 3."

Preparing for the Next Lesson:

When you have done the drills and a progress check as directed, you are almost finished for the day. Very quickly, make sure you are ready for Lesson 4. If you prepare your next lesson now, you will find it much easier to proceed when the time comes to actually do it. Be ready by having these items on hand:

- Pace card.
- Timer.
- "Progress" book.
- Drill book (light non-fiction with word counts complete).
- Clips.
- Scratch paper.
- Pencil.
- Calculator (optional).

LESSON 4

---Comprehension, Retention, and Recall---

Summary:

1. Reading at high speeds is of no value if you do not satisfy your purpose for reading. This is "adequate/satisfactory" comprehension.
2. Once we realize that the basic purpose of reading is to satisfy our own particular needs, we can shed the guilt associated with "not getting *everything*" out of the reading.
3. Working toward this end are three factors—comprehension, retention, and recall—the comprehension sequence. These are three distinctly separate but linked factors.
4. True comprehension is an individual process only the reader can determine. No two people ever see exactly the same meaning.
5. Carefully read, then do Drill 4.
6. Measure and record your progress.

General Concepts:

The term "comprehension" is perhaps the most maligned aspect of our reading process. In traditional terms, comprehension is very often wrongly defined, either explicitly or implicitly, as the process whereby we read material and can, at some later time, recount various bits of information from that reading. This implies that input, storage, and output are all lumped together in one absolute element. This is very misleading.

To understand the complex comprehension issue we must first recognize that there are three separate factors involved in making use of the ideas presented in written material:

- comprehension
- retention
- recall

These factors must not be jammed together under the single term "comprehension" as traditional reading methodologies tend to do. They are three separate links in the chain; and efficient readers must be able to see the uniqueness of each link as well as the bond that connects them together in a process better-termed the "comprehesion sequence."

Secondly, you must understand that every time you read you should be aware of whatever purpose it is you are trying to satisfy. Are you just killing time? Is this reading for pure entertainment? Do you need to "know" this material for a test or for your job? If you satisfy that predetermined purpose, your reading is definitely successful—you have adequate or satisfactory comprehension.

The Individuality of Comprehension:

1. Comprehension is the intangible recognition of how you, as a unique individual, relate to what you are reading at the exact moment you are reading it.

2. Comprehension is also taking what you already have inside you, intellectually and emotionally, and mixing it with what the author has to say. It is a sharing of ideas with the author. This assimilation process is the heart of comprehension—you make inferences and deductions and draw conclusions, you agree or disagree—all based on your individual makeup. You are reacting to the material being read.

3. No two people do this assimilation in the same way. We are each made up of a unique blend of morals, mores, interests, education, genetic traits, basic intelligence, vocabulary, experiences, ad infinitum. These very same factors that define each of us as unique individuals, also define us as unique interpreters of what we read. No two people ever "read the same book" because, when you mix that individual uniqueness with the ideas the author is presenting, the result is a one-of-a-kind combination.

4. For this very reason, comprehension cannot be measured. If you and I read a book, and I give you a test on it, you are being graded on your ability to blend with the author's ideas in the exact, same way that I think is correct or important. If twenty people read a book and each of them makes up a test on that book, how many different tests will you get? Twenty, of course! Everybody not only attaches varying degrees of importance to the material that is being

read but they also have infinitely divergent interpretations as they combine their individualism with the essence offered by the author.

5. Don't ever let yourself think that you are a less than capable reader because you didn't get the same ideas from a book that someone else did. This doesn't mean that you shouldn't study what the respected scholars think is the proper interpretation of a piece of writing. It simply means that if you didn't get the same ideas you are not a failure as a reader.

   Remember that class in poetry when the teacher asked what a poem meant and, after a number of students had presented various ideas, the teacher said, "No, that's not it! I'll tell you what it means."

   Isn't that nice—a psychic teacher. How does that teacher know what the poet was trying to say. Did they meet for coffee last hour in the cafeteria and discuss the poem? Or is the teacher merely repeating what the college literature professor said it meant. Better that the teacher should ask what each of several students think the poem means, then tell the class what one or several literary scholars think it means and, finally, wrap it up with a discussion about how these interpretations came to be without labeling any one as *the* correct meaning. Both academe and individuality are served.

   The more you study a subject, the more likely you are to realize that while many elements of interpretation in a book are common to a great many people, there are just as many, if not more, uncommon elements. Robert Frost was once asked the exact meaning of one of his lines of poetry. Frost thought for a moment and wisely replied, "When I wrote that line, God and I knew what I meant. Now, only God knows." Frost realized that he was no longer the exact same person who wrote those words and, as a result, his interpretation of them was now different. He did not feel that there had to be an absolute interpretation.

   John Steinbeck proffered a very similar viewpoint when, in an introductory note to *The Pearl*, he said, "If this story is a parable, perhaps everyone takes his own meaning from it and reads his own life into it." Notice how he even said, "*If* this story is a parable..." He is telling us that you can read it for whatever interpretation *you* want to put on it. There are no absolute meanings in literature. To search for the single meaning of a book is an act of folly; to find the many meanings is an act of wisdom.

Comprehension and Difficult Material:

Comprehension may be considered satisfactory even if the author has written material that is "over your head." Think for a moment, remembering that the key factor in understanding comprehension is recognizing that it is immutably tied to our *purpose* for reading. Suppose you had to read a book on astrophysics and had never studied science beyond the eighth grade. That book might not make a lot of sense to you. But if your sole reason for reading it was to report on its suitability for a beginning class in science, you could say you comprehended very well because you realized it was far too complicated for beginners. You were able to *satisfy your purpose* for reading it which was to determine its difficulty level. That satisfaction of purpose is adequate comprehension.

In a similar scenario, suppose you had that same meager background in science and you were given this same book to read as part of a general physics course in college. Your purpose for reading it would now be quite different than before, yet you could have adequate comprehension by simply recognizing there are many new concepts that you need to learn. The actual learning process is a totally *separate* step we will deal with in just a moment.

You do not have to understand every element of every idea when you read. All you need to do is note accurately the difficulty level of the material as it pertains to your present level of knowledge. If you can relate in this way, you have satisfactory comprehension. The problem, of course, is that this doesn't help you pass the tests in your physics class. Take heart, this precise relating of your knowledge to the author's is just step one. The second step in the process would be to determine just what material must actually be learned. And step three would be to learn it.

Read First—Learn Second:

Perhaps the most crucial rule in *Intensive Reading* with regard to the comprehension sequence is "*READ FIRST—LEARN SECOND*" (R1-L2). What this means is that you must never consciously work at learning *while* you are reading. Don't try to force it by repetition or regression. Just read and let the concepts fall where they may, even though you recognize that there is much learning needed if you are to make effective use of the ideas the author is presenting.

Once you have read the material—be it a section, a chapter, an entire book—you will *come back* to it and do your learning. You will be given some *very specific* tools to help implement this "read first, learn second" concept when you get to Lessons 6 and 8. Don't be impatient. Everything *will* fall into place.

Remember, the rule is to never consciously *try* to learn as you read. There will be a great deal of reading where your mind will be able to blend and mix with the author's ideas quite easily without your making a conscious effort to do so. This is called "incidental" learning. You will not have to work at it, yet you will come away with new concepts, conclusions, inferences, etc. Never try to force it. If you feel you are missing something and the ideas just don't mesh, you are under no obligation to learn on the spot. Save the learning till later. Read first for general concepts and merely get an idea of how you relate with the author; then *return* to do the learning of specific concepts and data. ***Read first—Learn second.***

Retention:

Retention is simply a part of what you often think of as memory. It is the mental storage of whatever information you get from a bit of reading. It can be aided in several ways:

1. **Good comprehension**, i.e., undertanding just how you and the author mesh and just what learning, if any, needs to be done to satisfy your purpose for reading.
2. **Using the new information** in some way—writing it down (study notes, etc.), discussing it with someone, or actually putting it to use (using a just-learned formula to figure out something).
3. **Using various mnemonics**—memory devices that aid retention and recall of information. Here are a couple very simple ones.
   - catchword—making a key word with the first letters from words on a list to help you remember the list. "H·O·M·E·S" helps you remember the names of the Great Lakes.
   - catchphrase—taking the first letters of words on a list and making up new words for those letters, arranging the words into a catchy phrase. "**E**very **G**ood **B**oy **D**oes **F**ine" helps you remember the notes on the lines of the music staff (E, G, B, D, F).

There are many other ways to help you improve your retention (and recall). They are far too numerous and detailed to be covered here. The best thing you could do in this regard would be to find one of the many good books written on memory techniques if you are interested in pursuing it further.

Recall:

Of the three links in our reading chain, recall is, by far, the weakest. But, fortunately for all of us, recall is a trainable skill and can be enhanced through proper practice and understanding.

Recall is the bringing back to conscious mind the information gleaned and stored from a past experience—in this case, reading. (Comprehension puts information into the brain, retention holds on to it, and recall brings it back.)

Too many times, when you can't "remember" something, you fault comprehension or retention; but it is really weak *recall* at fault. How many times have you insisted you "knew" the answer to a question but just couldn't dredge it out of the depths of your brain. As soon as someone gave you the answer, you realized immediately it was the correct one and you reaffirmed your contention that you did know it but just couldn't remember. The "couldn't remember" in that situation should be changed to a more accurate "couldn't recall."

Why do you think multiple choice tests are easier than fill-in-the-blanks? Because the multiple choice test, by giving several options, provides a "trigger" for the brain—a pathway for connecting with stored information. Without the clue, you might never be able to come up with the right answer.

Recall is nothing more than a conscious reaching into the subconscious for some bit of saved information, finding it, and bringing it to conscious recognition. It is a bridge between your conscious and your subconscious. You have a conscious need for information and a subconscious resource; you need to make the link between the two.

Like retention, recall can be aided with mnemonics and regular use of specific information so that the pathway to that part of the brain where the information is stored is a familiar trail. Recall is rarely taught as a specific skill in school and is even more rarely practiced or drilled. It can become very efficient with proper training wherein you build more and stronger bridges to span the gaps from those conscious needs to the subconscious resources.

Recognizing this requirement for recall practice will help you understand the need to include recall in your reading drills. It is the end-link in the chain. When you have strong recall skills you maximize the use of information stored in your brain. This in turn gives you confidence when you read because you then know that what you put into your mental storehouse will be available for withdrawal later on. This confidence breeds comfort and relaxation which in turn enhance comprehension. Enhanced comprehension increases the potential for good retention and recall. You create a positive cycle that continues to grow as your techniques and skills are sharpened.

Written Recalls:

In order to strengthen your recall skills, the drills for this lesson will utilize a written recall in addition to the basic pacing skills. The purpose of the written recall is to help teach your mind to make the connection between conscious need for information and subconscious storage of that data. When you put informaton into your brain during the drilling, you also want to practice bringing it back out. Because you are drilling at speeds that do not allow for adequate comprehension, you *will* get a feeling of missing things. This is very normal. What the recall exercises do is teach you to bring back as much as you can of whatever bits and pieces of information went in, whether they entered your brain consciously or subconsciously.

Because you are not able to subvocalize every single word in the way you've always done in the past, you may think little or nothing is going into your brain; but, in fact, quite a bit is going in. The problem is that much of the gathered information enters subconsciously so you don't have a chance to mull it over as it goes in. The recall practice will get you to realize that it's not the information input that is the problem; it's the recalling that needs more training.

Mr. Guilt:

Tied to all the misconceptions we've mentioned about comprehension, is a little gremlin who will sit on your shoulder when you are reading or drilling. This little character has a direct line to your brain and he keeps whispering, "You're not memorizing enough. Slow down and study more as you go. Sure, you're going fast but you're not learning anything."

Get rid of that little rascal, Mr. Guilt. *You do not have to try to learn as you read.* Remember, R1—L2! Plus, when you are *drilling*, satisfactory comprehension is not required nor is it even desired. If you are doing the drills but still getting satisfactory comprehension, you are drilling too slowly!

By the same token, when you are *reading*, you do not have to recall everything. You can read for pure entertainment. After all, if you go to a music concert and enjoy a symphony you've never heard before, do you sit there trying to memorize each note. Heavens, no! You enjoy it for the aesthetic uplift it gives you at the time. Why shouldn't some of your reading be the same way. There are times when you should be able to pick up a book, whether fiction or non-fiction, and read it for the sheer enjoyment it brings you at the moment. A week later, there is no need to recall everything about that book any more than there is a need for you to be able to whistle every note that you heard at the concert. Get rid of Mr. Guilt and enjoy reading knowing that you can read for pure enjoyment if you so choose.

You can, of course, also choose to read primarily for knowledge enhancement. When you do read for knowledge enhancement, let whatever seems to fall into place, fall into place; *then* come back and learn whatever else you want to learn. *YOU* make the decision, not Mr. Guilt. And, when you do get rid of Mr. Guilt, a nice positive cycle has a chance to expand significantly.

Lesson 4 Drills:

1. **Preparation:** Make sure you have made all the necessary preparations for the drills. Have at hand your timer, drill book, paper, pencil, clips, and the pace card as described in the Introduction.
2. **Recalls:** Carefully read Appendix 5 to understand how to do the written recalls that will be part of today's drills.

3. **Drilling:** Read through Drill 4. You will note that it is exactly the same as Drill 1 except that a written recall has been added as part of the procedure. After a careful read-through of the drill, do it very carefully paying close attention to your written recall process.

4. **Progress Record:** After doing Drill 4, take a timed, three-minute reading in your "progress" book, compute your speed and record it in Appendix 3 on the "Lesson 4" line. ***Be sure you are using your pace card!*** Push yourself at whatever you feel is your fastest speed that will still allow adequate comprehension. You are now *reading* not *drilling*.

5. **Preparing for the Next Lesson:** When you have done the drill and progress check as directed, make sure you are ready for Lesson 5 by having the usual drill items on hand.

"Nature does not demand that we be perfect
—it only requires that we grow!"

"Obstacles are those frightful things you see when you take your eyes off your goals!"

LESSON 5

---Reinforcing Speed and Recall---

Summary:

1. The concepts learned in Lessons 1 and 4 must be reviewed and then reinforced with more drilling.
2. Review Lesson 4 if necessary.
3. Read and then do Drill 5.
4. Read and then do Drill 6.
5. Measure and record your progress.

Note: Be sure to have all the necessary materials on hand when you start.

Review and Reinforcement:

1. In Lesson 4 you learned all about comprehension, retention, and recall; and how they fit into the picture of efficient reading. You also learned the prime importance of understanding that reading is a very individual process. Stop, now, to review what you know about these factors. If you feel fairly certain that you understand them clearly, you are ready to proceed. If you are not quite sure, go back to Lesson 4 and do a very rapid sweeping through the chapter—using your pace card, of course! (Just as you surely are using it now!) Remember, you *must* use your pace card every time you read! When you are satisfied with your grasp of the concepts covered in Lesson 4, proceed to the drills.
2. First read through, then do Drill 5. Be sure to include good written recalls as asked for in the directions. While this aspect of the drill may seem like mere "busy work" right now, be assured that it is extremely important. The little time and effort it takes to do the

recall will pay huge dividends in the form of increased confidence that comes from the doing the drill properly.

3. Preread carefully, then do Drill 6, keeping in mind the preceding admonishment about doing the recall portion properly.
4. Make a progress check using your "progress" book. Starting wherever you left off at the end of your last timed reading, set your timer for three minutes and read at your *best rate* using the pace card. ***Be sure to use your pace card from above!*** Pace at whatever rate you feel is the fastest you can go while still getting adequate comprehension. You are *reading* not *drilling*.

   At the end of the three minutes, mark your place and compute your speed just as you did before.

   Full pages x words per page = xxx words

   Lines on partial pages x words per line = xxx words

   total words

   divide by 3

   WPM

5. Mark your speed on the progress chart in Appendix 3, on the line, "Lesson 5."

Preparing for the Next Lesson:

When you have done the drills and a progress check as directed, you are almost finished for the day. Very quickly, make sure you are ready for Lesson 6 by having on hand all the usual materials *plus your non-fiction drill book*—with word counts complete.

LESSON 6

---The Organized Reading System---

Summary:

1. *Efficient* reading (speed plus effectiveness) depends, in a large part, on your ability to establish an effective *structure* for your reading.
2. The Organized Reading System (ORS) gives you this structure by dividing the reading process into five steps—*overview, preview, read, postview, and review.*
3. These steps are used in varying degrees according to your responsibility for the material and the difficulty level of the material.
4. Flexibility is the primary focus of this lesson, with efficiency the end-product.
5. Read through and then do Drill 7.
6. Measure and record your progress.

Beginning Note:

It is very important in this chapter that you heed the early admonition to *read through the entire lesson first*, then come back to study and learn the parts with which you need to spend more time. As you see how the ORS works, the "*Read first—Learn second*" (R1—L2) concept will fall neatly into place.

Why an Organized Reading System:

Would you embark on a long auto trip without consulting a road map? Would you dive into a pool without knowing the water's depth? And isn't grocery shopping a lot easier with a list? But how many times have you proceeded to read by simply starting at the first word and plodding on? Failure to read with some sort of organized approach is one of the most common, yet most severe, faults of the average reader. *Intensive Reading* has a solution to this problem.

The simplest and easiest way to set up an efficient and flexible approach to your reading is to use the ORS. It is something that should be used with *all* of your reading, not just the most difficult material. But, as you will see, ORS is not used to exactly the same degree every time you apply it. This is what makes it so effective—flexibility.

Understanding the Organized Reading System:

The ORS is divided into five individual and sequential steps, each of which is used ***only if needed.*** We will deal with each element in detail later in the chapter.

- **Overview**—A look at the physical characteristics of the material to be read (basic content; length; type size; noting of pictures, maps, charts, or diagrams; organization; etc.).
- **Preview**—A sweeping through the material at three to five times faster than a normal reading pace in order to get *just a thread* of the meaning.
- **Read**—The actual reading of the material at the reader's own *best rate*—the fastest pace possible while still maintaining adequate comprehension.
- **Postview**—A rapid sweeping through the material just read in order to tie up loose ends, reaffirm certain concepts and ideas, and learn any bits of information deemed important during the "read" segment.
- **Review**—A very rapid sweeping through the text at some later date in order to reacquaint the reader with the material and to reaffirm concepts.

As you read about each of the five sections in detail, note that, although the term "book" is used frequently in the instructions for ORS, you will use the same basic procedure in *all* kinds of material—memos, letters, magazine articles, etc. (More about this later.)

Also keep in mind that *you will not use every step every time you read.* Which step or steps you will use will be determined by two key factors: difficulty level and responsibility. Don't think that you will have to go through some long, arduous process every time you read.

After each separate step in the ORS has once been defined and explained, the entire sequence will be put together for you to show just how it can be utilized to your best advantage. ORS is very easy to use and takes only a short bit of time to apply, even if you go through all the five steps. It will take a few lessons and drills to get used to using ORS; but, when you have learned it, you will find that it becomes a tremendous time saver. The effort it takes you to learn how each step works will be another wise investment in your self improvement! As you go through this lesson (using your pace card!), keep in mind our frequently-mentioned rule: R1—L2. In other words, simply finish reading through this lesson without working at trying to learn, then come back and do any learning or studying you think needs to be done.

Overview:

The very first step in the ORS is the *overview.* It is the only one of the five steps that is ***always*** done. The purpose of an overview is to establish both non-text particulars and actual text format. This will give you a "road map" of the book (or memo, article, letter, etc.). It gives you a vague idea about the difficulty level, basic content, organization, and suitability to your needs. It will also give you your first ideas about the best way to actually read the book; if, in fact, you decide you really do want to read it.

1. Examine the cover, jacket, and title page looking for relevant non-text particulars such as:
   - Title
   - Author
   - Basic content, theme, or subject
   - Copyright date
   - Publisher
   - Jacket comments
2. Rapidly thumb through the entire book simply noting format details such as:
   - Length
   - Size and style of type

- Organization (Does it have . . .?)

chapters	sections and sub-sections
lessons	summaries
questions	exercises

- Pre-text material (just note whether or not these sections exist—don't attempt to read them during the overview)

preface	table of contents
introduction	author's note

- In-text enforcement aids (as with pre-text material, just note their presence)

maps	graphs
charts	diagrams
pictures	footnotes

- Post-text information (as above, just note the absence or the existence of these sections—don't read)

index	glossary
appendix	bibliography
endnotes	

3. Decide on your approach to reading the material by quickly answering such questions as:

   - Does the material look useful, enjoyable, or interesting; and should I, in fact, take the time and effort to read it?

     If the answer to the question above is negative, then get rid of the book and start on another. There are too many good books around to waste your time reading one that you really aren't sure you want or need to read. If, however you think you want to go on with the reading, then proceed to the next ORS step.

   - Does it look easy to read or difficult?
   - What is the largest, logical, cohesive section I could comfortably read at one time? An entire chapter? Perhaps a section? Only a sub-section? One paragraph?

4. In very short, or informal type of reading material such as a letter, memo, or news article, your overview will obviously not be as involved and may consist of no more than answering four very basic questions:
   - What's it about?
   - How long is it?
   - Who wrote it?
   - Do I need or want to read it?

Preview (Non-Text Material):

Once you have made the decision to go ahead with the reading, even though it may be a somewhat tentative decision, you are now ready to preview the non-text material.

1. Sweep through the first section of non-text information at *three to five times faster* than you can read it with adequate comprehension. This will give you a minimal idea of what the material is about.
   - If this thread of content piques your interest and it looks worth the time to actually *read*, then go ahead and *read* it at your own *best rate*.
   - If the thread of content does not appear interesting enough to warrant *reading*, move on to the next non-text section.
2. When you have completed previewing each of the non-text sections, you must use whatever information you gleaned to decide on your approach to the actual text. Based on what you perceive to be the difficulty level of the material and taking into account your responsibility for learning the content, break up the text into the largest, logical, cohesive units you think you can handle.
   - For a book that looks relatively easy to read, you may decide that you can easily handle a whole chapter at a time.
   - If the material appears more difficult, or, if you have a lot of learning to do, you may decide to take just a section or even a sub-section at a time.

Preview (Text):

1. Sweep through the first unit of text (chapter, section, sub-section, etc.) at a rate three to five times faster than your "normal" rate in order to merely get a *thin, outlined idea of the content.* As you do this quick pace-through of the text section, take note of things such as author's style, the main theme or thesis, vocabulary level, etc.

   Note: If you have decided to tackle an entire chapter at a time, you may simply read the section headings (if the material is divided that way); or, sometimes, there may be a summary or even a set of section-ending questions which you could quickly read to get the content thread. These strategies would preclude the three-to-five-times-faster sweeping through the material.

2. Now, once again, assess the value of the text material.
   - If the text does not appear to deliver the information you need, skip it and go on to the next chapter, the next article, the next book, etc.
   - If the text appears to have what you do want or need, go on to the next preview step.

3. Begin questioning the material (anticipation), making use of what *you* can contribute in terms of prior knowledge of the subject, familiarity with the writer, interest in the subject, your responsibility for the content, etc.

4. Consciously recognize your purpose for reading (learning, pleasure, information, study, etc.).

Read:

"Read" is just exactly as the name implies. Using your pace card from above, of course, you push yourself at the best possible rate for your own comfort and confidence, taking one logical section at a time.

If you have a high responsibility for learning the content, *do not try to learn as you read.* Read for what you can get at the time you are reading. You will come back to do the learning when you are in the postview step. (R1—L2, remember!)

Note: It must be mentioned here that a distinct part of the "read" procedure in most material is the use of the *Margin Code System*. We will learn all about it in Lesson 8. Don't worry about it now. Just know that we will cover it as an indispensable aid to the learning process. It will give you the confidence to move through the "*read*" step without Mr. Guilt shouting inside your head. Right now, all you are to be concerned with is learning the basic procedures involved in ORS. Fine tuning the skill will come later.

Postview:

After you have read the material, an *optional* next step in ORS is "postview." If, when you have finished reading, you feel as though you have accomplished your purpose for reading and have gotten satisfactory comprehension, you may consider your reading process complete and quit at this point. However, if there are loose ends to tie up, or there are major areas of learning to be done, you will want to move into the postview mode.

A postview may be done in one of two ways, or you can even combine the two. The first method would be to take a very general look at the material just read in order to consolidate a few ideas or to simply reinforce what you just got out of the reading. It is done by sweeping through the material at three to five times faster than your normal rate just as you did in the preview; or by just reading section or sub-section headings, summary, or questions (as you might have done in the preview).

The second way you can postview is to take a detailed look at very specific sections of the material in order to study, learn, or otherwise digest the information contained therein. This is done by going back to whatever section(s) caused you problems in understanding and doing whatever is necessary to satisfy your responsibility and purpose.

During this time, you might reread, write notes, memorize, mull over or study, etc. This is also the time when you will want to highlight or underline the information deemed most important. The Margin Code System, while not absolutely necessary, can play a very important role in a specific postview. You will be able to tie Margin Coding to the ORS when you get to Lesson 8.

Review:

A "*review*" is very much the same as a "*postview*" except it is separated from the other four ORS steps by a gap in time—a day, a week, a month, etc. It allows you, at any later time, to return to the material and make a quick survey of it to jog your recall system to see if you are still comfortable with the ideas and information presented. If not satisfied, you may feel you need to reread, in which case the "review" actually turns into a "preview" and you continue through the rest of the steps just as you did the first time around.

Using the Organized Reading System:

Let's take a look at how to use the ORS by running through an example. We mentioned earlier that the ORS is a very flexible system and that all five steps need not be applied every time you read. The only absolutely required step is the first one, overview.

Suppose you pick up a book you think you want to read; the first step, as we just noted, would be an overview. After the overview, you ask the question, "Do I still want to read it?" If not, put the book aside and move on to something else. But, if you decide you want to stick with it, you now have a choice: do you think a preview is worthwhile or should you just jump into the read step. If reading is your choice, go ahead and do it. If, however, you feel the need to preview because of the difficulty of the material or your high responsibility for material content, do the preview.

After the preview, based on the additional information you now have about the book, you again ask the question, "Do I want to continue?"

If the answer is "no," quit and move on. If the answer is "yes," re-evaluate your breakdown of the material into the largest, logical cohesive units you can handle. This may be a chapter, or a section of a chapter, or even just a paragraph of exceptionally difficult material. Take the first unit and decide just as you did before, "Should I preview it first and then read it, or should I jump directly to the read mode?" When you have completed the read mode, decide if you want to postview; and, if so, what type of postview is best.

Proceed through each of the units in this manner until you have finished the book. The key to using the ORS is two-fold. First, be sure you understand each step as a separate procedure—what does it accomplish and how is it done?

Second, understand that only step one, *overview*, is absolutely required in every type of reading. The rest is strictly optional. Anytime after the overview you may abandon the material as being without merit for your purposes, or you may jump to a read mode. You may also abandon the material anywhere along the line if you feel you have, at that point, gained all that you need—to go on would be a mere reiteration of already-known information and therefore an inefficient use of time and effort.

As your responsibility for the content increases, or as the difficulty level of the material increases, there should be a correlative increase in the amount of time you spend prereading (overview and preview) and postreading (postview and review).

Figure 1, "Flexibility Chart," p. 40, illustrates this concept. Note that at the very bottom of the chart representing very low responsibility and/or easy-to-read material, there is virtually no prereading or postreading. Then, as the difficulty level and/or the responsibility factor increases, the time spent on prereading and postreading efforts must also increase.

The important thing to remember about the ORS is that, while it provides a distinct, organized structure to your reading, it is not cumbersome and absolute in its application. It is, instead, very flexible and personal. Right now, because it is new and you have not had a chance to drill in ORS, it seems like a lot of fussing and fiddling and you'd probably rather just read. Try to think of it as the road map we likened it to at the start of the lesson. Without a map, if you just set out in the general direction of your destination (which may not even be well-defined), you might be lucky enough to get where you think you want to go. In the chancy process, however, you most likely will drive many more miles than necessary taking wrong routes and detours; plus, you probably won't get an opportunity to see all the sights that you want to see.

But, if you use a road map and plan your trip carefully, you will not waste miles and time; you can see all the sights you want; you can change your route easily to avoid detours and delays; and you can readjust your schedule to spend more time in some places that you enjoy and less time in places that aren't so much fun.

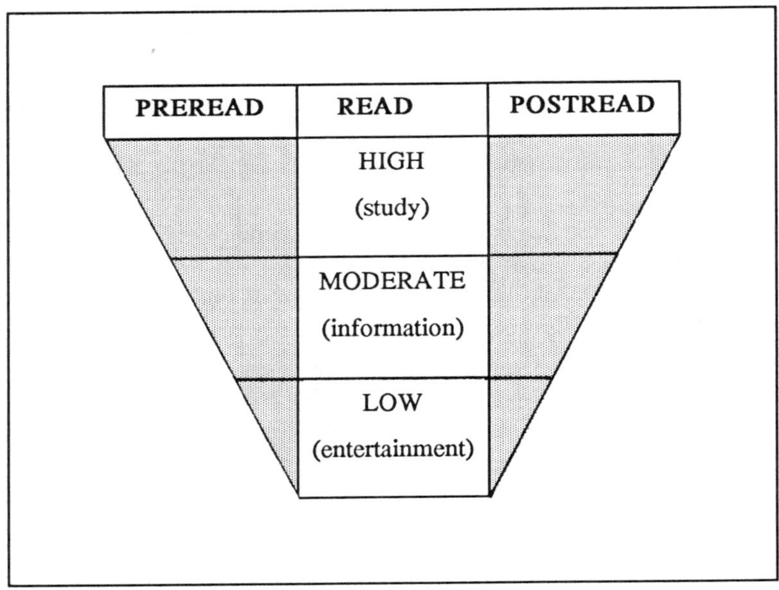

FIGURE 1—Flexibility Chart

Without the map, you are at the mercy of too many uncontrollable factors and you depend too heavily on chance; but, with the map, you can plan an itinerary, taking control of the trip so that it ends up providing you with the enjoyment you set out to achieve. You fulfill your purpose by getting where you want to go while seeing and enjoying those things you choose to see and enjoy along the way. You have organization, flexibility, and satisfaction. That's efficiency!

Reading needs a similar sort of a road map if it is to be equally efficient; and the ORS is that map. Make use of it every time you read.

Note: At this point you may want to postview this lesson to make sure you have it "locked in." When you are confident that you have the concepts well in hand, you may proceed with the drill.

Drilling in ORS:

Turn to the drill section at the back of the book and read Drill 7. After you have read the drill completely, actually do it.

Progress Record:

Using your "progress" book, do another timed, three-minute reading. Compute your speed and record it as "Lesson 6" in Appendix 3. Don't be surprised if you level off a bit in speed. Later, as you become more familiar with the *Intensive Reading* techniques, you will relax and tend to pay more attention to ideas than to procedure. This familiarity with the concepts will begin to show and your speed will increase dramatically. As long as your rate is at least double your beginning rate, you are doing just fine. If less than double, give Mr. Guilt another kick in the pants and push yourself a little harder. Drill speed must come first. Comprehension ***will*** follow.

Note: When you have finished this lesson, you will be well past the halfway point in the program. You might want to take note, also, that three of the four "content" lessons will have been done. Only one content lesson and three drilling lessons to go. It takes a lot of personal drive to stick with a self-learning program such as this is. Give yourself a lot of praise for following through so well. You have made a lot of progress—keep up the good work!

Preparing for Lesson 7:

Just a quick reminder of what should be a habit by now—have on hand all your materials for Lesson 7 so you can jump right into it tomorrow.

"When you read,
the universe is your domain!"

"Excuses are the nails used
to build a house of failure!"

LESSON 7

---Reinforcing ORS ---

Summary:

1. The ORS concepts learned in Lesson 6 must be reviewed and then reinforced with more drilling.
2. Read through, then do, Drill 8.
3. Do any one of Drills 4, 5, or 6.
4. Pay particular attention to the written recalls.
5. Measure and record your progress.

Review and Reinforcement:

In Lesson 6, you learned all about the Organized Reading System and how it can make your reading decidedly more efficient. Flexibility was emphasized, noting the foolishness of cover-to-cover reading of everything you start.

Since you now know what a *review* is, go back to Lesson 6 and formally review it. When you feel confident in your grasp of the ORS, go on to the prescribed drills for this lesson. (Remember, you must use your pace card every time you read!)

Procedure:

Make sure you have all the needed materials at hand before you begin. Keep in mind the importance of doing the drills exactly as directed, especially the written recalls. When you have done the drills and taken a progress reading, you are finished for today. You are now on the downhill side of the *Intensive Reading Program*. There is only one "learning" lesson left; the other two are review and drill. You are ever so close to making your reading as efficient as it can be. Pat yourself on the back for making it! Don't let up, though. These last lessons are very important to the fine tuning of your new skills. Keep the intensity and determination flowing until all ten lessons are finished and you have achieved a most noteworthy goal!

Drilling:

- Read, then do, Drill 8.
- Review, then do any one of Drills 4, 5, or 6.
- Pay particular attention to the written recalls.

Progress Record:

Using your "*progress*" book, do another three-minute reading from wherever you stopped reading last time. Compute your speed and record it as "Lesson 7" in Appendix 3.

Preparing for Lesson 8:

Now is the time to make sure all the usual materials are on hand for tomorrow's lesson. Be sure you have both *fiction and non-fiction* drill books handy as well as a couple of magazines of the type you normally read. *Reader's Digest* is an excellent drilling medium.

> "Habits are at first cobwebs,
> and then cables!"

LESSON 8

---Learning Difficult Material---

(Using the Margin Code System)

Summary:

1. In order to facilitate the "learn second" tenet of *Intensive Reading*, you must devise your own personal set of symbols to be used in the margins of your reading material.
2. These symbols will flag which items you want to learn or otherwise return to when in the postview mode. They will also indicate the *reason* for returning.
3. Read through and then do Drill 9.
4. Measure and then record your progress.

Why the Margin Code System:

Throughout the previous seven lessons, you have been told about a margin coding technique that will help the learning process when you have difficult material or material for which you have a high learning responsibility. The purpose of this Margin Code System (MCS) is two-fold: first, it relieves your brain of the responsibility of trying to learn as you are reading. This means that your brain is more relaxed and your incidental learning will be enhanced significantly. (Incidental learning is the kind of learning that takes place without your formally studying or memorizing the information.)

The second purpose for margin coding is to give you an organized method for returning to that material which you do need to learn or have high responsibility for. The codes not only tell you *what* to return to, but, if done correctly, will also tell you *why* you want to return.

The MCS can be an especially effective and efficient learning tool whenever the reader has a responsibility to "learn" the material. This responsibility will vary with each reader depending in great part on the type of reading being done. Such reading might include study material for classwork or professional improvement; work-related material such as memos, corporate reports, journals, and correspondence; or high-interest material for hobby or special personal use.

Using the Margin Code System:

The MCS is no more than a series or set of symbols devised by you, the individual reader, that will tell you exactly what to do with each marked section when you come back to do the postview. Suppose, as you are reading, you realize that the section you are reading has some value for you and you need to look at it more closely. The MCS then tells you to mark the margin with a symbol so you can return to that section when you are in the "*Learn second*" (postview) phase of your reading process.

You do not want to stop your reading midstream to deal with learning. Mark your code in the margin and move on through the material. When you have finished the entire section you had determined was the most logical "chunk" you could read at one time, you do a postview by coming back to each marked section and dealing with it according to the code you had assigned it. (We'll get to the code symbols themselves in just a minute.)

Margin Code Rules:

Although there are only six basic rules to MCS, you must learn these six rules and adhere to them precisely. As with all aspects of *Intensive Reading*, if you try to shortcut the rules or procedures you are not going to get the benefits promised; and you will be doing a great disservice to both *Intensive Reading* and yourself. The six basic tenets are:

1. Use only symbols that mean something to you.
2. Use only symbols that are easily remembered. This "remembering" is reinforced tremendously by repeated and consistent use.
3. Use at least three different symbols. You must have some sort of discrimination to tell you precisely what you are to do with the marked material. Do not use just one catch-all check mark.

4. At first, limit the total number of symbols to those you will use regularly. Too many symbols will only confuse you. Five symbols are usually more than enough to start with; seven is definitely tops.

   Note: Later on, when you are in the habit of using all of the *Intensive Reading* techniques and are comfortable with the margin codes, you can certainly add as many as you find useful to you.

5. Use the system on a regular basis so its application becomes a habit and the codes are automatic. You do not want to waste time trying to decide which symbol is needed.

6. Don't hesitate to revise your set of symbols as the need arises. Your purpose for reading as well as the type of material you are reading will differ from time to time making it necessary to add, delete, or otherwise change your codes.

Suggested Symbols and Meanings:

Any set of symbols that you devise must be ones *you*, as a unique individual, see as logical. The following suggested codes are only for example's sake. If, however, you find they fit your pattern of thinking, use them. Otherwise, devise your own symbols with your own special meanings. The kind of material and the reasons for reading it will do more to determine your code than anything else. A psychology major in college will have far different needs than a computer operator in a brokerage firm. So also will the doctor differ from the homemaker, the secretary from the lawyer.

At any rate, here are some *suggested* symbols. Use any or all that make sense to you and devise others to fill out your special needs.

X = very important (perhaps should be highlighted?)

√ = may be important (check it later)

? = confusing (reread it later?)

% = important statistic

V = valuable data

Q = quote worth noting

M = to be memorized

A = viewpoint to be mulled over (I agree with the author)

D = viewpoint to be "debated" (I disagree with the author)

B = bibliography information or footnote of value

df = definition to be looked up

ex = good example or analogy

Just as there are an infinite number of reasons for reading, so are there infinite possibilities for codes. The important thing is to devise your very own master set of symbols and use them religiously. Once you have turned MCS into a habit, you will see your confidence soar when reading difficult material because you no longer have Mr. Guilt as a nagging companion.

Library Books, Etc.:

There are bound to be times when you are reading a book or other material in which you do not want to make any marks; e.g., library books, precious volumes, borrowed material, etc. A way to overcome this obstacle is to simply get one or two of the very small sticky pads (e.g. 3M's Post-It pads) and stick a little square wherever you need to write in the margin. This is a minor inconvenience compared to writing directly on the page itself, but it does protect the book while still allowing you to read more efficiently with the use of the MCS.

A Note on Highlighting or Underlining:

There will be many circumstances when you will want to underline or highlight portions of what you are reading. This is just fine, **BUT,** instead of doing it *as* you read, put a special symbol in the margin. Then, during your postview, go back to the sections with this "potential-highlight" code and review them to see if, in fact, you really want to highlight now that you have read the entire selection and can weigh the relative value of the marked section.

How many times have you just gone ahead and highlighted as you read, thinking, "Hmm, this looks interesting; this looks important;

better highlight this; and that, too." By the time you finished the chapter, it was 98% highlighted. Proper margin coding will eliminate this problem by letting you truly discriminate between the important and the not-so-important.

Drilling:

The drilling to reinforce the MCS is quite simple, especially since you are well-acquainted with several different drill procedures by now. Drill 9, although a new drill, is done very much like to other drills and should not be a problem for you at all. It is a magazine drill that uses the ORS which adds the responsibility of putting in appropriate margin codes during the "*read*" portion of the drill. As you did with each of the previous drills, read through the instructions first, then return to do the drill step by step.

You may turn to Drill 9 now, read through it, and then do it. When you have done the drill, return here to finish the lesson.

A Final Reminder:

Make the MCS a personal system that you know and use without hesitation. Its effective application will most definitely improve your reading efficiency and, therefore, your confidence. This is a significant part of that positive cycle you want to generate.

Progress Record:

Do another "progress" reading, noting the speed in Appendix 3 on the line marked "Lesson 8."

Preparing for Lesson 9:

You are getting very close to the end now. Having gone through all of the "learning" lessons, you now need only to bear down and reinforce what you have learned. Don't make the disasterous mistake of thinking you can stop now or just coast for two lessons. This is the fine tuning part of the program coming up.

The next two lessons are where you really can make giant strides in speed and confidence if you follow the procedures exactly and put some real enthusiasm into what you are doing. Don't succumb to the temptation to ease up in the home stretch.

"TRY?

There is no try!

There is only do or not do!"

LESSON 9

---Turning Intensive Reading into a Habit---

Summary:

1. All of the *Intensive Reading* concepts learned in the previous lessons must be reviewed and then reinforced with more drilling.
2. Review and then do Drill 9.
3. Review and then do any two of Drills 4, 5, or 6.
4. Pay particular attention to the written recalls.
5. Measure and record your progress.

Review and Reinforcement:

If there is any part of the *Intensive Reading* concept that you do not feel totally comfortable with, now is the time to go back and review that section. When you feel that you have a thorough understanding of the methodology, it is time to put forth a real push in your drilling to get your speed up where it can be and to lock in the techniques as a habitual way of reading.

Procedure:

Make sure you have all the needed materials at hand before you begin. Keep in mind the importance of doing the drills exactly as directed, especially the written recalls. When you have done the drills and taken a progress reading, you are finished for today.

Drilling:

- Review, then do Drill 9. Pay very close attention to using the MCS properly all the while still pushing for speed.
- Review, then do any two of Drills 4, 5, or 6. Relax and make a big push for speed, always keeping in mind that

when you are in a *drill* mode you do not need nor do you even want adequate comprehension.

- Also pay close attention to the written recalls.

Progress Record:

Using your "progress" book, do another three-minute reading from wherever you stopped reading last time. Compute your speed and record it as "Lesson 9" in Appendix 3.

Preparing for Lesson 10:

Well, it is getting mighty close to the end. Just one big lesson left. You have worked hard to get here; now, keep it up for a big spurt in your next and final lesson.

"What we are to be
we are now becoming"

LESSON 10

---The Final Touches---

Summary:

1. As with any skill, your mastery of *Intensive Reading* depends on reinforcement of the concepts and techniques.
2. Review and then do Drill 9.
3. Review and then do any two of Drills 4, 5, or 6.
4. Pay particular attention to the written recalls.
5. Measure and record your progress.
6. Compute your net word gain as well as the percentage gain for the entire *Intensive Reading Program.*

Review and Reinforcement:

If there is any part of the *Intensive Reading Program* that you do not feel totally comfortable with, take the time now to review it and lock it in. Don't look at a review as mere busy work. The benefits gained by reinforcing the theories as well as techniques are more than worth whatever time it takes to do it. Remember, you are establishing a habit here and habits come from repetition. Keep up your drive for excellence in this last lesson.

Procedure:

Make sure you have all the needed materials at hand before you begin. Keep in mind the importance of doing the drills exactly as directed, especially the written recalls. When you have done the drills and taken a progress reading, you may do a final comparison between your beginning rate and your ending rate to see just what you have achieved. And, when that is done, you should take a quick look at the final chapter in this book, "A Lifelong Skill."

Drilling:

- Review, then do Drill 9. Pay very close attention to using the MCS properly all the while still pushing for speed during the *Read* portion of the drill.
- Review, then do any two of Drills 4, 5, or 6. You may do, for instance, two Drill 4s, or one Drill 4 and one Drill 6.
- Relax and make a big push for speed, always keeping in mind that when you are in a *drill* mode you do not need nor do you even want adequate comprehension.
- Also pay close attention to the written recalls.

Progress Record:

Using your "progress" book, do a final three-minute reading from wherever you stopped reading last time. Compute your speed and record it as "Ending rate" in Appendix 3.

Net Gains:

If you have understood the concepts and followed the drill procedures exactly as directed, you already know without any measurements that you have advanced considerably in your reading efficiency. Nonetheless, it is nice to know in very objective terms just how much you have accomplished.

Subtract your "Beginning rate" from your "Ending rate" to find your net wpm gain. This tells just how many more words per minute you are reading. Then divide this net word gain by your "Beginning rate" to find out your percentage of improvement.

Example: Suppose you had an "Ending rate" of 570 wpm and a "Beginning rate" of 215 wpm.

570 - 215 = 355 wpm **gain**

355 ÷ 215 = 165% **gain**

(You are reading over two and a half times faster!)

A JOB WELL DONE!

A LIFELONG SKILL

---Making Intensive Reading a Habit---

The Value of Continued Drilling:

The lasting power of any skill is directly related to your use of that skill and to your continued efforts to improve. Thus, your newly acquired reading skills can be quickly diminished if you do not use them every time you read. Putting this new-found ability to work for you will become a totally subconscious process if you use the techniques religiously, i.e., ***every time you read.***

You can also continue to ***improve*** your speed and effectiveness with additional drilling. These additional drills take so little time and effort on your part that it would be very foolish not to set up a moderate drill schedule for the next four to six weeks. You will be refining an amazing level of reading efficiency that will last a lifetime.

One absolute, unequivocal quarantee can be made—if you don't hone this skill now, you will, at some later date, most surely bemoan the neglect. You will, one day, find yourself in a situation where a perfected reading skill will be of inestimable value and the skill that might have been, won't be. You will utter those rueful words of regret, "If only I had . . . ."

So, don't be one of those who came so close to the prize but gave up because of the extra effort needed to make the final surge. The drill regimen is far from rigorous and can be accomodated in everyone's schedule. Don't debate it or argue about it, just tell yourself that you are worth every bit of effort expended, then set your goal and do it!

The Drill Schedule:

If you do a lot a reading, personal or professional, during the course of a day, and, if, in that reading, you incorporate all the techniques you have just learned, you will need less drilling than one who does very little reading. Most likely, though, you wouldn't have stuck with this program if you didn't do a lot of reading.

With that in mind, **the general rule of thumb is to do at least three drills per week for the next four weeks.** If you have the intestinal fortitude to do more (say, six drills per week for six weeks) by all means do so. If you can, spread the drills out so that you do one drill every other day or one drill every day. Don't bunch them and do, for instance, all three drills in one evening. However, if bunching is absolutely the only way you can get the drills in, then do it; but, if you have a choice, spread them out.

The Drills Required:

Drill specifics are really quite simple. You should, of course, use common sense to modify the program, wherever necessary, to fit your particular needs better. Here is the basic formula to follow.

- Review the drill quickly before you do it.
- Do any two of Drills 4, 5, or 6. Any combination is fine.
- Do Drill 9.

One Last Word:

You have taken a tremendous step in self-improvement. You are in total control of how much more you might accomplish. Don't make excuses and don't sell yourself short. The lifelong skill of efficient reading is a major accomplishment only a relatively few people ever achieve. Be one of those elite! Be master of your fate!

You must determine what you need from reading and then read to satisfy that purpose. Reading is an individual process that only ***you*** can properly control. Time and again it has been shown that readers are leaders! **The world is yours if you read.**

"It is necessary to try to surpass oneself always; this occupation ought to last as long as life!"

APPENDIX 1

---Choosing Your Drill Books---

General Criterion:

Do not pick a book you have "always wanted to read." The personal need to "understand everything" in such a book is much too high and frustration will set in too easily. There is a little gremlin called "Mr. Guilt." He attacks your brain with comments like, "So what if you drilled at 600 wpm, you didn't get *every possible* bit of information!" By picking a book in which you have no responsibility for the content, you will be denying Mr. Guilt a stranglehold on your brain.

Fiction Criteria:

Choosing fiction books for drilling is really very easy. There are only three criteria:

- **Simplicity**—This is the most important factor. You must choose a book that has a very simple literary style and structure, i.e., an uncomplicated plot with a limited number of characters. You'll be much more comfortable with a simple plot line and just a few characters that you can easily follow, even though you are drilling.
- **Appeal**—Choose a simple book of the type or style that generally appeals to you (western, thriller, romance, etc.). This general appeal is an obvious asset in two ways: first, you are more likely to stick to a good drill regimen if you are interested in the book you are using; and, second, you will not have to work so hard to get something out of it if you have an interest in the material to start with.
- **Lack of Responsibility**—As noted before, make sure the book is one in which you have *absolutely no responsibility* for content, i.e., you have no committment to learn or study the material. If you get something out of it, fine; if not, that's okay, too. As you get more acquainted with the

techniques of *Intensive Reading*, you can "upgrade" your choices according to your own good judgement.

Non-Fiction Criteria:

Non-fiction book selection is based on the same principles as fiction selection:

- uncomplicated data
- information in an area of general interest
- zero responsibility for the content

Suggested Titles:

Sometimes it is helpful to have specific examples rather than just some general guidelines. With that in mind, here are some ideas for you as you look for books to use in this program.

- **Fiction**—The fiction books listed below are excellent examples of good drill books in that they have a general appeal and they fit the easy-style criteria for drilling. This is by no means a complete listing—merely a smattering of excellent possibilities.

The Pearl	*The Old Man and the Sea*
Old Yeller	*Sink the Bismarck*
Shane	*When the Legends Die*
Tom Sawyer	*The Ox-Bow Incident*
The Red Pony	*The Red Badge of Courage*
Call of the Wild	*Good-bye, Mr. Chips*
White Fang	*To Kill a Mockingbird*

- **Non-Fiction**—It is extremely difficult to list good examples of non-fiction books because personal interest and individual base of information play such key roles in the selection process. Also, the technical, scientific, or topical information contained in some of these books can become outdated very quickly. However, two titles do crop up as good, reasonably "timeless" examples:

Psycho-Cybernetics *Think and Grow Rich*

General Notes:

It would be wise to select several books at one time so that you have a ready replacement in case the first one you drill in proves unsuitable. Plus, you will find, as you progress, that you will eat up enormous chunks of material in one drill session and may well finish several books in the course of the ten *Intensive Reading* lessons.

If you finish a book and find that the content was very interesting and you would like to go back and get more satisfactory comprehension, don't hesitate to drill through the same book a second time; especially if you are doing different types of drills. Repetition of material in drills is perfectly all right. In some cases it may actually be advantageous because your acquired knowledge of the material allows you to relax more and let the system work for you. Mr. Guilt will not be able to gain a foothold in your brain. With that in mind, you might consider as a drill book one that you enjoyed reading once before.

Recap/Reminder:

Take care that you choose a topic in which you have high interest; yet, be sure it is a book with easy-to-read content for which you have little or no responsibility.

> "If the only tool you have is a hammer,
> every problem looks like a nail!"

"Learn from the mistakes of others—
you can never live long enough
to make them all yourself!"

APPENDIX 2

---Computing Words Per Page---

General Caution:

It is vital to the flow of the drills that you do your "arithmetic" ahead of time. This means to compute average words per page of each book well before you use it for drilling. This will leave your practice time free to concentrate on the drills.

Procedure:

While the actual word counting is quite easy, the overall procedure can be confusing to some people. If you read the directions carefully and follow them exactly, you should have no trouble getting accurate counts.

- **WPL (Words Per Line)**—Count the number of words in ten arbitrarily chosen full length lines. Count *each* word regardless of length. Then compute the average number of words per line.

  Example: The total word count for ten full lines is 94. Then divide 94 by 10 to get **9.4 wpl.**

- **LPP (Lines Per Page)**—Determine the average number of lines per page by first counting the number of full lines. Then estimate how many full lines the partial lines would be roughly equal to. Add these two figures to get total full lines per page. Do this for three pages and find the average.

Example: You have turned arbitrarily to any page and have counted the *full* lines which equal 28. Then by looking at the remaining *partial* lines you have estimated them to be the *equivalent* of about 3 full lines. Then, these results would be added together for a total of **31** lines.

Then you would turn arbitrarily to another page and do the same to get a total, perhaps, of **33** lines.

A third page might yield **32** lines.

Adding all three totals to give you a grand total of **96.**

Dividing this total by **3** results in an average of **32 lpp** .

31 + 33 + 32 = 96 ÷ 3 = 32 lpp

- **WPP (Words Per Page)**—Multiply the words per line by the lines per page to get the average number of words per page.

wpl x lpp = wpp

Example: Using the numbers derived in the two previous examples, we would have an equation like this:

9.4 x 32 = 301 wpp

"Mediocre people are always at their best!"

APPENDIX 3

---Personal Progress Record---

As you proceed through the ten lessons of *Intensive Reading*, you will want to keep a record of your progress. Do not think that each time you record your rate it will necessarily be higher than the previous rate recording. It may fluctuate quite a bit because you are introduced to different types of drills in different kinds of material for each of the lessons. Even though you have set aside one book just for your progress readings, rates may still vary. Don't fret about it. The overall trend of your reading rates will go up and by the end of the ten lessons you will have doubled or even tripled your speed easily. You will feel the progress you are making. The rate record is just a visible notation of that achievment.

Beginning rate = ...191.... wpm

Lesson 1 rate = ... wpm

Lesson 2 rate = ... wpm

Lesson 3 rate = ... wpm

Lesson 4 rate = ... wpm

Lesson 5 rate = ... wpm

Lesson 6 rate = ... wpm

Lesson 7 rate = ... wpm

Lesson 8 rate = ... wpm

Lesson 9 rate = ... wpm

Ending rate = ... wpm

"To conquer without risk
is to triumph without glory!"

APPENDIX 4

---Vertical Pacing Exercise---

NOTE: The faster you read, the more vertical your pace becomes. Your eyes will take in more words per fixation meaning fewer fixations per line. This, in turn, means your eyes will move more quickly down the page. To demonstrate how your eyes learn to soften their focus and widen their fixation span, read the article about the sinking of the ship Titanic that begins on the next page. Use your pace card and read down the columns from start to finish as rapidly as you can while maintaining satisfactory comprehension.

If you are curious about your speed in this columned reading, time yourself. Using a watch, clock or stopwatch, note *exactly* how long it takes you to read the whole story. Convert the minutes and seconds to decimal equivalents of minutes (each six seconds equals .1 minute). Divide the total words (830) by your time to get words per minute.

> **Example:** Suppose it took you 2 minutes and 18 seconds to read the article. The decimal equivalent would be 2.3 minutes. Divide 830 by 2.3 to get a speed of 361 wpm.

Turn the page, start your timer and read the article.

The Titanic

On the evening
of Monday,
April 14, 1912,
one of the
greatest tragedies
ever to occur
in maritime
history
sent a wave
of disbelief
through the
entire world.
That night,
1,522 men,
women, and
children
either drowned
or froze to death
when the Royal
Mail Steamship
Titanic struck
an iceberg and
sank in the
North Atlantic.

Although much has
been written about
this catastrophe,
little note has
been made about
America's involvement
nor of the Senate
inquiry that followed.
As soon as word
reached the shores
of America that
the "unsinkable" ship,
the Titanic, had

actually foundered, stories about the sinking were instantly and irresponsibly generated. A few were based on sketchy facts and the rest were merely figments of the writers' imaginations.

In order to separate the facts from the fancy, Senator William Alden Smith of Michigan headed a sub-committee to inquire into the entire affair. Just two days after the Titanic's demise, the inquiry held its first session, subpoenaing witnesses from among the 713 survivors, nautical experts, and others.

Testimony from the ship's owners, her officers and crew, and from the unlucky passengers led to a trail of mistakes of unbelievably huge proportions. All the testimony seemed to point to one, grave, inescapable fact —the loss of lives would have been minimal, maybe even zero, if only the gross negligence of many persons had not created the tragic situation.

Repeated warnings that numerous icebergs were in the area and dangerously close to the Titanic's path were ignored with total disdain. The ship even ran at its top speed during that fateful night.

The lookout, against all logic, did not even have a pair of binoculars to use and was able to spot the villainous iceberg at only the last possible second. At this final moment of impending doom, the officer at the helm panicked, turning the ship broadside to the advancing juggernaut. In just ten seconds, an underwater spar from the iceberg had neatly sliced a 300-foot gash in the Titanic's side as if the thick steel plating were nothing more than a biscuit tin. Almost every single nautical expert who testified agreed that had the Titanic rammed that iceberg head-on, even at her top speed, she would have suffered no more than a bone-jarring crash and a crumpled bow.

Because the Titanic's skin had been so easily sliced, few passengers or crew even knew something had happened. At this point, warnings should have been given to the passengers to prepare to abandon ship, but no such alarm was given. Only when the ship was listing noticeably did the officers and crew begin to herd some of the passengers into the lifeboats. Then, compounding error upon error, the boats were not filled to capacity. Some lifeboats, capable of taking on 65 persons, held as few as 14—a disproportionate number of them being crewmen rather than passengers.

Distress rockets finally fired by the Titanic were seen, recognized, and then aloofly disregarded by the captain of another ship, the Californian, less than ten miles away to the north.

Even as the Titanic sank beneath the icy waves, dumping its hundreds of victims into the frigid waters, a great share of survivors in lifeboats heartlessly ignored the impassioned

pleas and terrified shrieks
of the less fortunate who were
left adrift, doomed to face
a slow, agonizing death in
the bitter, frozen void of
the North Atlantic.

In contrast, some genuine
acts of courage and heroism
did appear. Women refused
to board lifeboats when they
realized their husbands were
to be excluded—preferring
instead to face death at their
husbands' sides. Some crewmen
and even some of the passengers
nobly gave up their life jackets
to the less fortunate who hadn't
had time to retrieve their own.

The captain of another ship, the
Carpathia, responded immediately
to the short frantic call for help
on the wireless. At great risk to
his own ship, he steamed full
speed toward the foundering
Titanic. The Carpathia was the
only ship to pick up survivors
—713 lucky souls.

The Titanic's band did in fact
stand on the listing deck of
the doomed ship playing music
to the very last. But, it should
be noted, they were playing
"Autumn" not "Nearer My God to
Thee" as is popularly believed.

As a result of the Senate Inquiry, several pieces of maritime legislation were enacted. These laws spelled out in detail the requirements for the number and capacity of lifeboats, the need for regular lifeboat drills and individual assignment to a specific boat, the operating requirements for wireless radio, and procedures for the use of distress rockets. It was then, also, that the United States Coast Guard was inaugurated; and shipping lanes were moved sixty miles farther south to avoid the threat of ice.

Yes, some good did come of the Titanic's sinking and the terrible loss of lives; but it was too steep a price to pay for a lesson in common sense and a respect for fellow man.

* * *

"We cannot grow
if we will not change!"

"Those who say it can't be done
often get in the way
of those who are doing it!"

APPENDIX 5

---Written Recalls---

In order to foster effective recall, you must, as with any skill, train yourself to do it well. As a part of your regular drill procedures, you will be asked to do a written recall to get you used to "remembering" more and more of what you read. Included in this appendix are three suggested formats for written recalls. It is very important that you do not underestimate the value of these written recalls.

- **The *patterns* are critical** in that they train your brain to think of recalled items in some sort of connected fashion. Rather than just listing remembered information one item after the other, you must put down the main idea and the subordinate ideas in some way that shows the relationships pictorially--thus the patterns. Use only key words and phrases; do not write in complete sentences. Use any kind of connecting line you want to show that one fact or idea relates to another fact or idea (or several other ideas).

- **Do not spend a lot of time** on the written recall segments of the drill. Quickly jot down whatever you can easily recall, then move on to the next step of the drill. Each recall step should take less than a minute. Don't wrack your brain for every last possible scrap of information. It is the act of recalling that is important, not the quantity or quality of the recall.

- **Keep adding** to your recall until it becomes too loaded to add to or until the story line shifts and you have another main idea to deal with. No two people will ever do a recall exactly the same way, so don't worry about the "correctness" of it. As long as you have put the ideas into some pattern that makes sense to *you*, you are doing it correctly. Unlined, 8 1/2" x 11" paper seems to work the best.

---SAMPLE PATTERNS---

Slash:

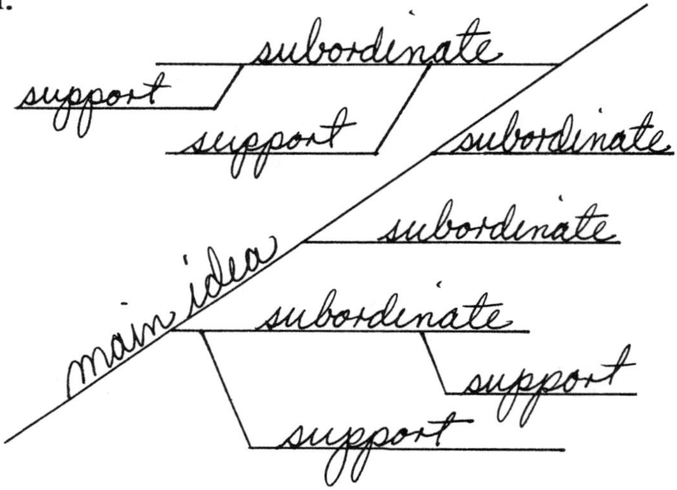

subordinate
support
support
subordinate
subordinate
main idea
subordinate
support
support

Linear:

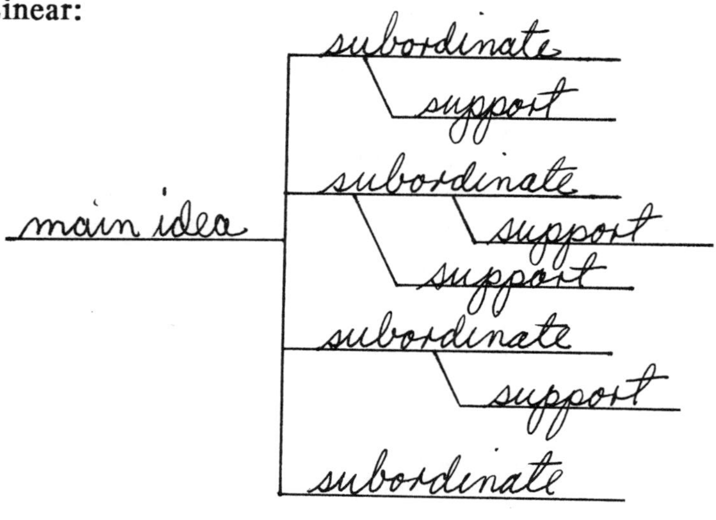

main idea
subordinate
support
subordinate
support
support
subordinate
support
subordinate

Radial:

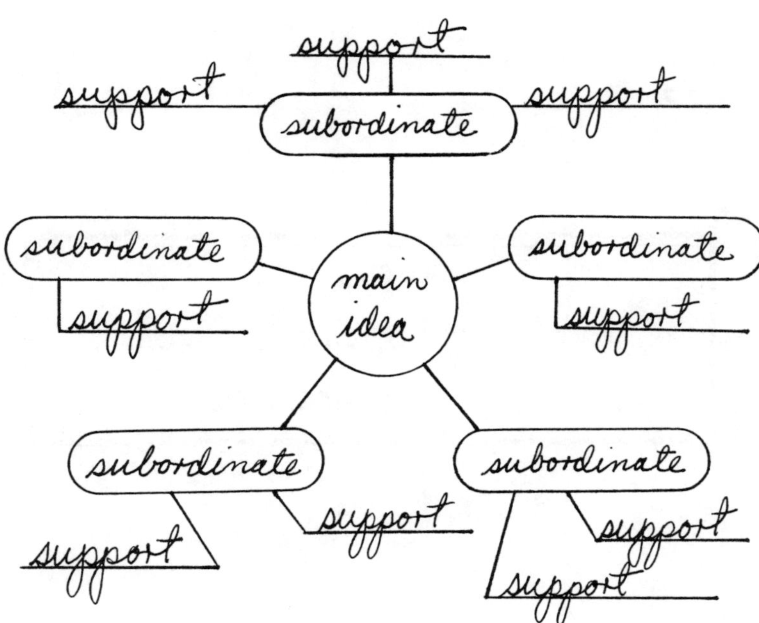

“Chance favors the prepared!”

"A person's mind,
once stretched by an original idea,
never regains it's original dimensions!"

DRILL 1

Objective: basic, raw speed increase

Time alloted: approximately 30 minutes

Material used: light fiction

General Instructions:

1. Be sure you have your timer on hand.
2. Be sure that you have selected your drill book according to the instructions in Appendix 1 and have done the word counts as directed in Appendix 2.
3. Read through the entire drill before you do any of it.
4. After the read-through, do each step as directed.
5. Be sure to use your pace card from above.

Drill Procedure:

1. Read into new material for five minutes. ("New material" means to start at the very beginning of a new book or pick up wherever you left off if you have already started the book.) Use your pace card from above, of course, and read at a pace that gives you *adequate comprehension*. Mark your beginning and ending places.
2. Add one-third the number of pages you just read. Then, in five minutes, pace through the entire section (the pages read in step 1 plus the just-added pages).

Example: In the first five-minute reading you covered page 1 through page 6. (A total of six pages read.)

$$6 \div 3 = 2$$

You would then add two pages to the original six making an eight-page section from page 1 through page 8.

$$6 + 2 = 8$$

➡ Push yourself to make it through the marked section in the allowed time. If you finish before your timer beeps, don't go any farther. Instead, drop back to the first page of the section and start through a second time pushing until the time is up.

➡ Remember that you are now *drilling* and comprehension is not a concern. If you get something out of it fine; if not, that's fine, too. Relax and just let it flow. You'll have to suspend your concern for story line or content and concentrate on a pace that's fast enough to make it through the entire section in five minutes. Just because you cannot subvocalize every word as you have been used to doing, don't despair. The drill is designed to push you at speeds much faster than you can adequately subvocalize. Remember, we are not killing off comprehension; we are merely setting it aside for a short time while we concentrate on pacing and speed.

3. Now add another increment (the same number of pages as added in step 2). Pace through the entire section in five minutes.

Example: Step 1 had you *reading* pages 1-6. Step 2 added two pages and you then *paced* through pages 1-8 in five minutes. Now add two more pages (same number added in step 2) to make a section of pages 1-10. Set your timer for five minutes, start it and pace through pages 1-10 in the alloted five minutes. If you don't make it all the way through in the five minutes, simply resolve to push fast enough to make it next time.

4. Add another increment (same number of pages added in step 2 and again in step 3). Pace through the entire section in five minutes.

   Example: Step 1 meant pages 1-6. Step 2 meant pages 1-8. Step 3 meant pages 1-10. Now, you will have a section covering pages 1-12.

5. Go on to your next drill, if required by the directions in your Lesson, or go back to the Lesson to finish up for this session.

> "Ignorance: an equal opportunity destroyer!"

"Good, better, best–
Never let it rest;
Till the good is better,
And the better is best!"

DRILL 2

Objective: basic, raw speed increase

Time alloted: approximately 20 minutes

Material used: light fiction

General Instructions:

1. Be sure you have your timer on hand.
2. Be sure you have selected your drill book per instructions in Appendix 1 and have done the word counts as directed in Appendix 2.
3. Read through the entire drill before you do any of it.
4. After the read-through, do each step as directed.
5. Be sure to use your pace card from above.

Drill Procedure:

1. Read into new material for seven minutes. Use your pace card, of course. Push for speed but still maintain a *reading* pace that gives you adequate comprehension. Mark your beginning and ending places.
2. Pace through *the same material you just read*, but do it in just *five* minutes. Remember that an acclimation to pacing is our primary focus. If you are going so fast that you can't subvocalize every word, you are doing the drill correctly.
3. Pace through the same material in four minutes.
4. Pace through the same material in three minutes.
5. (Optional) If you really want to give yourself a challenge, pace through the same material in just two minutes.

Note: Concern yourself only with the quality of your pacing from above. In Steps 2-5, if your eyes seem to be "hopscotching" around grabbing a word or two here and a phrase or two there, don't fret—that's perfectly normal.

6. Go on to your next drill or go back to the Lesson to finish up for this session.

"Hats off to the past;
coats off to the future!"

DRILL 3

Objective: basic, raw speed increase

Time alloted: approximately 20 minutes

Material used: light fiction

General Instructions:

1. Be sure you have your timer on hand.
2. Be sure you have selected your drill book per instructions in Appendix 1 and have done the word counts as directed in Appendix 2.
3. Read through the entire drill before you do any of it.
4. After the read-through, do each step as directed.
5. Be sure to use your pace card from above.

Drill Procedure:

1. Mark off a new section in your drill book equal to seven times your *best rate* (this means the fastest you can go and still get adequate comprehension).

   Example: If you read comfortably at 400 wpm, mark off a section of 2800 words.

   7 x 400 = 2800

2. Pace through the marked section in just two minutes. Yes, that is very fast! But remember, all you have to do is focus on *seeing* the words—you do not need nor even want adequate comprehension! Concentrate on good pacing technique and let whatever happens, happen. Remember, you are *drilling*. Let your eyes sweep across the line of words beneath your pace card. Just because you cannot subvocalize every word, don't panic and let Mr. Guilt get to you. Your eyes are, in fact, seeing all the words and transmitting them to

your brain even though much, if not all, of the process is subconscious. This is exactly as it should be!

3. Pace through the same section in three minutes.
4. Pace through the same section in four minutes.
5. Pace through a final time in five minutes.

> **Note:** Concern yourself only with the quality of your pacing from above. In Steps 2-5, if your eyes seem to be "hopscotching" around grabbing a word or two here and a phrase or two there, don't fret—that's perfectly normal.

6. Go on to your next drill or go back to the Lesson to finish up for this session.

> "Impossible is a word to be found only in the dictionary of fools!"

DRILL 4

Objective: speed reinforcement and recall practice

Time alloted: approximately 30 minutes

Material used: fiction

General Instructions:

1. Be sure you have your timer and recall materials (pencil and paper) on hand.
2. Be sure you have selected your drill book per instructions in Appendix 1 and have done the word counts as directed in Appendix 2.
3. Read through the entire drill before actually doing it. Note that this drill procedure is the same as the procedure for Drill 1 except *we have added a written recall.*
4. After reading through the drill, do each step as directed.
5. Be sure to use your pace card from above.

Drill Procedure:

1. Read into new material for five minutes. Use your pace card from above, of course, and read at *your best rate*—the fastest you can go and still get adequate comprehension. Mark your beginning and ending places.
2. Start a written recall as described in Appendix 5. Be sure to use one of the suggested patterns. Don't worry about the correctness of your recall. Use key words or phrases and make connections wherever you can. As soon as you have to "stretch" for more recall, stop writing and go on to the next step in the drill.
3. Add one-third the number of pages you just read in Step 1.

Example: Suppose, in the first five-minute reading you covered a total of nine pages.

9 ÷ 3 = 3

You would then add three pages to the original nine, making a total marked section of 12 pages.

9 + 3 = 12

➡ Now, pace through the entire 12-page section in five minutes. Push yourself to make it in the allowed time. If you finish before your timer beeps, don't go any farther. Instead, drop back to the first page of the section and start through a second time pushing for speed until the time is up.

➡ Remember that you are now *drilling* and comprehension is not a concern. If you get something out of it fine; if not, that's fine, too. Relax and just let it flow. You'll have to suspend your concern for story line or content and concentrate on a pace that's fast enough to make it through the entire section in five minutes. Just because you cannot subvocalize every word as you have been used to doing ever since learning to read, don't despair. This drill is designed to push you at speeds much faster than you can adequately subvocalize. Remember, we are not killing off comprehension; we are merely setting it aside for a short time while we concentrate on pacing and speed.

➡ When the timer does go off, return to your written recall and add as much information as you can, as quickly as you can. Don't fret about neatness or correctness at this point—just get it down on that recall in some patterned fashion.

4. Now add another increment (the same number of pages you added in Step 2).

Example: In Step 1, you read nine pages. In Step 2, you added three more. Now add another three.

9 + 3 + 3 = 15

- ➡ Pace through the entire 15-page section in five minutes. Push your pace to make sure you finish in the alloted time.
- ➡ If you finish the section ahead of your timer, don't stop to wait for the timer; and don't go on into new material. Instead, go back to the beginning of the 15-page section and start through a second time.
- ➡ As soon as your timer goes off, go to your recall and add, as fast as you can write it, any additional recall information you can think of.

4. Add another increment (same number added in Steps 2 and 3).

Example: Step 1 covered nine pages. Steps 2 and 3 each added three more pages. Now we'll add another three.

9 + 3 + 3 + 3 = 18

- ➡ Pace through the full 18-page section in five minutes. Push your pace so you finish in the alloted time.
- ➡ If you finish ahead of your timer, don't go on into new material. Instead, go back to the beginning of the 18-page section and start through a second time.
- ➡ As soon as your timer goes off, return to your recall and add, as fast as you can, any additional recall information you can think of. Be sure to pattern it.

5. Go on to your next drill or go back to the Lesson to finish up for today.

"It makes little difference how many
university courses or degrees people may own;
if they cannot use words to move an idea
from one point to another,
their education is incomplete!"

DRILL 5

Objective: speed reinforcement and recall practice

Time alloted: approximately 20 minutes

Material used: light fiction

General Instructions:

1. Be sure you have your timer and recall materials (paper and pencil) on hand.
2. Be sure you have the appropriate drill book and have done the word counts as directed in Appendix 2.
3. Read through this entire drill before you do any of it. Note that it is the same as Drill 2 except for the *added written recall.*
4. After the read-through, do each step as directed.
5. Be sure to use your pace card from above.

Drill Procedure:

1. Read into new material for seven minutes. Use your pace card, of course. Push for speed but still maintain a *reading* pace that gives you satisfactory comprehension—your *best rate.* Mark your beginning and ending places.
2. Start a written recall as described in Appendix 5.
3. Pace through the *same material you just read,* but do it in just five minutes. Remember that an acclimation to pacing is our primary focus.
   - If you are going so fast that you can't subvocalize every word, you *are* doing the drill correctly.
   - Don't concern yourself with where your eyes are in relation to the pace card. They may be on the line immediately below the pace card or they may be three or four or six

below the pace card or they may be three or four or six lines ahead. Just tell yourself to *see* all the words and let your inner control do it's own thing subconsciously.

- If you reach the end of the section before the timer goes off, go back to the beginning of the section and start through a second time.
- When the timer goes off, immediately add to your recall.

3. Pace through the same material in four minutes and add to your recall.
4. Pace through the same material in three minutes and add to your recall.
5. (Optional) If you really want to give yourself a challenge, pace through the same material in just two minutes and add to your recall.

Note: Concern yourself only with the quality of your pacing from above. In Steps 2-5, if your eyes seem to be "hopscotching" around grabbing a word or two here and a phrase or two there, don't fret—that's perfectly normal.

6. Go on to your next drill or go back to the Lesson to finish up for this session.

"It's a poor mechanic
who blames the tools!"

DRILL 6

Objective: basic, raw speed increase

Time alloted: approximately 20 minutes

Material used: light fiction

General Instructions:

1. Observe that this drill is the same as Drill 3, except we have *added the written recall.*
2. Be sure you have your timer, drill book, and recall materials.
3. Read through the entire drill before you do any of it.
4. After the read-through, do each step as directed.
5. Be sure to use your pace card from above.

Drill Procedure:

1. Mark off a new section in your drill book equal to seven times your *best rate.*

   Example: If you read comfortably at 400 wpm, mark off a section of 2800 words.

   7 x 400 = 2800

2. Pace through the marked section in just two minutes.

   (Yes, this is very fast! But remember, all you have to do is focus on *seeing* the words. Concentrate on a good, smooth pacing technique and let whatever happens, happen. Remind yourself, you are *drilling.* Let your eyes sweep across the line of words beneath your pace card. While you cannot *subvocalize* every word, your eyes *are* seeing them and transmitting them to your brain even though much of the process is subconscious.)

3. When the timer rings, immediately start a written recall.
4. Pace through the same section in three minutes; add to your recall.
5. Pace through the same section in four minutes; add to your recall.
6. Pace through a final time in five minutes; add to your recall.

> **Note:** Concern yourself only with the quality of your pacing from above. In Steps 2-6, if your eyes seem to be "hopscotching" around grabbing a word or two here and a phrase or two there, don't fret—that's perfectly normal.

7. Go on to your next drill or go back to the Lesson to finish up for this session.

"Most people, on the average,
utilize only a fraction of their natural abilities–
that's why they're average!"

DRILL 7

Objective: reinforcement of ORS

Time alloted: approximately 30 minutes

Material used: light non-fiction

General Instructions:

1. Be sure you are using a very easy-to-read book of non-fiction for which you have absolutely no responsibility to learn.
2. Be sure you have your timer, drill book, and recall materials.
3. Read through the entire drill before you do any of it.
4. After the read-through, do each step as directed.
5. Be sure to use your pace card from above.

Drill Procedure:

1. Overview the entire book, noting as you go the presence or absence of the various pre-text and post-text elements listed in Lesson 6.
2. Start a written recall.
3. Go to each of the pre-text and post-text sections and do an overview and then a preview of each section.

> **Note:** The preview may be a sweeping through the full section at three to five times your normal pace; or, it may be a quick reading of the section headings, the summary, or questions at the end, if they exist.

4. Add to your recall.

5. When you have finished prereading the book overall, go to the first chapter and mark off anywhere from two to four sections of three to five pages each. The length and number of units will depend on the size of the chapter.

6. Proceed with the ORS in each of these units.

   - **Overview** the unit—add to your recall.
   - **Preview** the unit—add to your recall.
   - **Read** the unit at your *best rate*—add to your recall.
   - **Postview** the unit—add to your recall.

7. Repeat the above four ORS steps in each of the other marked units.

8. **Review** all of the units together—add to your recall.

9. Return to your lesson and continue with any other required drills or do the Progress Reading.

> "One of these days
> is none of these days!"

DRILL 8

Objective: reinforcement of ORS

Time alloted: approximately 30 minutes

Material used: light non-fiction

General Instructions:

1. Be sure you are using a very easy-to-read book of non-fiction for which you have absolutely no responsibility to learn.
2. Be sure you have your timer, drill book, and recall materials.
3. Read through the entire drill before you do any of it.
4. After the read-through, do each step as directed.
5. Be sure to use your pace card from above with a nice, smooth pacing movement.

Drill Procedure:

1. If not already done, overview the entire book, noting, as you go, the presence or absence of the various pre-text and post-text elements listed in Lesson 6.
2. Start a written recall.
3. Go to each of the pre-text and post-text sections and do an overview and then a preview of each section.
4. Add to your recall.
5. When you have finished prereading the book overall (or if you had done it in a previous drill), go to the first chapter or to a portion of the text you haven't read before and mark off a section equal to eight times your *best rate.*

Example: You feel very comfortable at 400 wpm in this material so you mark off a section of 3200 words.

8 x 400 = 3200 words

6. Proceed with the ORS in the marked section.
   - **Overview** the section—20 seconds maximum—and start or add to your written recall.
   - **Preview** the section—90 seconds maximum—add to your recall.
   - **Read** the section—5 minutes maximum—add to your recall.
   - **Postview** the section—90 seconds maximum—add to your recall.
7. Return to your Lesson and continue with any other required drills or readings.

"Discipline is remembering what you really want!"

DRILL 9

Objective: reinforcement of speed, ORS, and MCS

Time alloted: approximately 20 minutes

Material used: magazine of general interest (e.g., *Reader's Digest*)

General Instructions:

1. Be sure you are using a magazine you like to read.
2. Be sure you have your timer, drill book, and recall materials.
3. Read through the entire drill before you do any of it.
4. After the read-through, do each step as directed.
5. Be sure to use your pace card from above with a nice, smooth pacing movement.

Drill Procedure:

1. By title alone (or short annotation if available in table of contents), choose two short articles of interest to you.

   Note: If you are using Reader's Digest, you may want to note that there are about 40 words per column inch, 250 words per full page column, and 500 words per full page (two full columns). This 40 words per column inch will be a reasonable assumption for most narrow columns in other magazines and newspapers, too.

2. Assume a hypothetical responsibility for the content of the article, e.g., you need the material as a basis for a report you must write.
3. Based on this responsibility, devise a personal set of margin codes according to criteria set forth in the two sections of Lesson 8 titled "Margin Code Rules" and "Suggested Symbols and Meanings."

4. *Preread* the first article, i.e., do an *overview* and a *preview*. This should take only a few seconds and in many cases, common sense will tell you to combine the two steps if the article is fairly short and easy to read.

5. *Read* the first article at your *best rate*. Make a push for speed. During this portion, however, also use the margin codes to mark those sections you feel you would want to come back to for further "study." Remember, it will help give your brain a focus if you have assigned yourself a hypothetical responsibility for the content, as suggested in Step 2.

> **Note:** Don't spend any extra time on this *read* step—no rereading, no regressing, no trying to learn, no repetition, etc. Remember, you are to *READ FIRST* (this step)—*LEARN SECOND* (next step).

6. *Postview* the article by going back to deal with the sections you had margin-coded. During this step you are to do the learning, mulling over, debating, etc. Highlight portions if warranted.

7. Return to your Lesson and continue with any other required drills or reading.

> "I bargained with life for a penny
> and life would pay no more!"

GLOSSARY

---Acronyms---

IRP = Intensive Reading Program—A system of skills and techniques that allows you read any kind of material at the fastest possible rate in order to get what you want to get out of it.

LPP / lpp = lines per page.

MCS = Margin Code System.

ORS = Organized Reading System—a five-step, sytematic approach to reading effectiveness. The steps are overview, preview, read, postview, review.

R1—L2 = Read first—Learn second.

WPL / wpl = words per line.

WPM / wpm = words per minute.

WPP / wpp = words per page.

---Definitions---

adequate comprehension = getting whatever you want out of the material. Same as "satisfactory comprehension."

auditory reassurance = hearing the words inside your head as you say them silently while reading. The "flip side" of subvocalization.

best rate = your fastest reading rate that will still allow adequate comprehension.

card pacing = using a card as a guide during the entire reading process, with the card coming down from above the line(s) being read.

comprehension = an intangible sharing of ideas with the author at the exact moment of reading. Does not *necessarily* include retention and recall. It is just one link in the comprehension sequence.

comprehension sequence = comprehension, retention, and recall —three links in the chain of learning through reading. Each of these factors is a separate, though connected, entity.

drilling = pacing through material at a speed faster than will allow for adequate comprehenison.

margin coding = a system of marking symbols in the margins as you read, thus relieving your brain of the responsibility of trying to learn as you read and also providing a guide for your postview or review process.

overview = a very rapid look at the overall, physical characteristics of the material you are contemplating reading.

pace card = a card of most any size used to guide your eyes rapidly down the page. It is used from above the line(s) to be read. (The exact card size to be used is determined by the needs and comfort of the individual reader. Business-card size or 4" x 2" blank cards are good general purpose pacers.)

postview = a sweeping through the material you just read for clarification or learning of either specific or general ideas. Very often aided by the use of margin codes.

preread = overview plus, possibly, a preview.

preview = a rapid sweeping through the material about to be read to see if it suits your needs or to see if it warrants actually *reading*.

reading = pacing through the material at the fastest possible rate that will still allow adequate comprehension.

review = a rapid sweeping through material some time after it has been read to refresh your mind and retrigger your recall.

satisfactory comprehension = getting whatever you want out of the material—satisfying your purpose for reading (entertainment, information, directions, or literary experience). It is the same as "adequate comprehension."

subvocalization = saying the words silently to yourself as you read them—the "flip side" to "auditory reassurance."

sweep = pace rapidly.

ABOUT THE AUTHOR

Dr. Goetzman has been in the training and education field for over twenty-five years. He began as a high school teacher and later became involved in adult education. His deeply-ingrained love of reading led him to analyze the characteristics of "good" readers, the reading process, and the teaching of reading. The result of this investigation was the formulation of an advanced literacy program designed to upgrade almost anyone's reading skills by a considerable margin. This *Intensive Reading Program*, as it was called, was put into a workshop format and Dr. Goetzman began teaching it in adult education classes and corporate training sessions. The results, over the years, have been dramatic—for thousands of people it has meant an average increase in reading speeds of over 150% in just a few short hours of training. People were reading two and a half times faster than they did before they were exposed to *Intensive Reading*. It is understandable why he has become known as "The Reading Doctor."

Dr. Goetzman recently completed an in-school session of *Intensive Reading* for third graders with equally outstanding results—average percentile rankings rose from 51 to 84 on the National Achievement Test in just eight weeks!

As a full-time speaker and trainer, Dr. Goetzman devotes his time to presenting workshops, seminars, and speeches. In addition to the *Intensive Reading Program* ("Making Molehills Out of Paper Mountains"), his workshops and speaking topics cover not only the entire literacy spectrum, but also motivation, self-image, thinking skills, education reform, and effective teaching.

CONTACTS

For additional information concerning Dr. Goetzman's programs, to check on his availability to present a speech or workshop for your company or organization, or for any other help he might be able to provide you, please contact Dr. Goetzman at:

Professional Resource Center

2028 17th Avenue NW

Rochester, MN 55901-1514

1-507-282-0941

1-800-848-4912, ext. 2675